Marseille Travel Guide 2025

Discover Iconic Landmarks and Essential Tips for an Unforgettable Trip to France's Mediterranean Gem

Anne Jesus

Copyright © 2024 by Anne Jesus

Table of Contents

Introduction: A Glimpse into Marseille

From the moment I set foot in Marseille, the city seemed to embrace me with its Mediterranean warmth. The air was thick with the scent of sea salt and spices, and as I entered the lively Vieux-Port, I immediately sensed that Marseille was more than just another city on the map—it was an experience waiting to unfold. Sunlight shimmered on the harbor, reflecting off the colorful boats, while fishermen proudly showcased their fresh catch to passersby. It was the kind of scene that lingers in your memory long after you've left.

Strolling through the winding alleys of Le Panier, Marseille's oldest neighborhood, I was captivated by the vibrant murals and street art that seemed to capture the city's eclectic and free-spirited vibe. Each turn revealed something new—charming cafés, local craft shops, and lively conversations drifting out from every open doorway. And when I finally reached the top of Basilique Notre-Dame de la Garde, the view was breathtaking—Marseille's terracotta rooftops stretched out to meet the sea, and I could feel the city's deep-rooted history all around me.

This guide is more than a list of places to visit—it's about truly experiencing the soul of Marseille. Whether you're here to immerse yourself in its rich history, explore its unique culture, or marvel at the stunning natural beauty of the Calanques, Marseille will leave its mark on you. Let this guide be your companion as you uncover the city's hidden gems and embrace the unforgettable spirit of Marseille—a place where every street has a story and every moment holds a discovery.

How to Use This Guide

This travel guide is crafted to help you make the most of your time in Marseille, whether you're here for a weekend getaway or an extended stay. Each chapter is organized to provide you with essential information on getting to Marseille, exploring its top attractions, dining in the best spots, shopping, and experiencing the vibrant local culture. You'll find insider tips on hidden gems, local customs, and the ideal times to visit each location. Practical advice is included on how to get around the city, stay connected, and manage your budget, with costs and prices mentioned where relevant. Whether you're carefully planning your itinerary or looking for some last-minute inspiration, this guide will be your go-to resource.

So grab your guide, pack your essentials, and get ready to uncover all the wonders Marseille has in store!

Chapter 1: Overview of Marseille

Marseille, the second-largest city in France, is a vibrant and historic port with a stunning Mediterranean coastline and a diverse cultural mix. Known for its charming old port, eclectic neighborhoods, and delectable seafood, it provides visitors with an authentic and lively experience. Whether you're drawn by its sunny beaches, ancient landmarks, or bustling markets, this guide will help you uncover the best of this southern French gem.

History of Marseille

Originally established by Greek sailors around 600 BC, Marseille, then called Massalia, stands as one of Europe's oldest cities. Its prime location on the Mediterranean made it a key trading hub, connecting Europe with the East. Over time, it absorbed influences from various civilizations like the Romans, Saracens, and Normans, contributing to its unique character.

During the French Revolution, the city became famous for "La Marseillaise," a song that later became the national anthem of France. Marseille thrived during the 19th and 20th centuries, with industrial growth and waves of immigration adding to its rich cultural fabric. Today, it's a dynamic city where ancient ruins coexist with modern life. Visitors can admire historical sites such as the Old Port (Vieux-Port) and Fort Saint-Jean while also enjoying the vibrant energy of the city center.

What Makes Marseille Famous?

1. The Vieux-Port (Old Port): The Old Port is the beating heart of Marseille, filled with fishing boats, yachts, and bustling cafes along the waterfront. Once a major trading post, it's now a lively area brimming with restaurants and markets. Strolling along the port at sunset is an essential experience for anyone visiting the city.

2. The Calanques National Park: Nestled between Marseille and Cassis, the Calanques boast a dramatic coastline where rugged limestone cliffs dive into the clear blue sea. Popular activities include hiking scenic trails or taking a boat tour, with prices ranging from €25 to €30 for a trip from Marseille to the Calanques.

3. Notre-Dame de la Garde: Perched high above Marseille, this basilica offers stunning panoramic views of the city and the Mediterranean. Locals affectionately call it "la bonne mère" (the good mother), believing it protects both the city and its sailors. Entry is free, though a small donation of around €5 is appreciated.

4. Bouillabaisse: No trip to Marseille is complete without sampling bouillabaisse, a famous fish stew made from a variety of local Mediterranean fish simmered in a rich broth. Prices for this dish range from €35 to €60 per person, depending on the restaurant.

5. Château d'If: Made famous by Alexandre Dumas' novel *The Count of Monte Cristo*, this former fortress and prison sits on a small island off the coast. Ferries to the island cost around €11 for adults and €5.50 for children.

6. Cultural Diversity: Marseille's multicultural essence is one of its most distinctive features, with influences from North Africa, Italy, and other Mediterranean regions evident in its markets, food, and festivals. To experience this diversity firsthand, visit during the annual Festival de Marseille, which showcases dance, music, and theater.

7. Football (Soccer): Football is a big passion in Marseille, and the city's team, Olympique de Marseille, is among France's top clubs. Attending a game at the Stade Vélodrome during a match is an unforgettable experience, with ticket prices ranging from €15 to €80 depending on seating and the game's significance.

Quick Facts about Marseille

- **Country:** France

- **Region:** Provence-Alpes-Côte d'Azur

- **Population:** Approximately 870,000 (as of 2023)

- **Language:** French (English is widely spoken in tourist areas)

- **Currency:** Euro (€)

- **Time Zone:** Central European Time (CET) | UTC +1 (Winter), UTC +2 (Summer)

- **Climate:** Mediterranean, featuring hot summers and mild winters

- **Main Airport:** Marseille Provence Airport (MRS)

- **Known for:** The Old Port (Vieux Port), Basilique Notre-Dame de la Garde, Château d'If, Bouillabaisse, Calanques National Park

- **Popular Dishes:** Bouillabaisse (fish stew), Pastis (anise-flavored liqueur), Navettes (traditional biscuits)

- **Major Events:** Fête de la Musique (June), Festival de Marseille (Summer), Christmas Market (December)

Essential French Phrases for Travelers

These useful French phrases will help you navigate Marseille and engage with locals:

Greetings & Basic Phrases:

- Hello: Bonjour (bohn-zhoor)

- Good evening: Bonsoir (bohn-swahr)

- Goodbye: Au revoir (oh ruh-vwah)

- Please: S'il vous plaît (seel voo pleh)

- Thank you: Merci (mehr-see)

- Yes: Oui (wee)

- No: Non (noh)

- Excuse me: Excusez-moi (ehk-skew-zay mwah)

- Sorry: Désolé (day-zoh-lay)

Asking for Help:

- Do you speak English?: Parlez-vous anglais? (par-lay voo ahn-glay)

- I don't understand: Je ne comprends pas (zhuh nuh kohm-prah pah)

- Can you help me?: Pouvez-vous m'aider? (poo-vay voo may-day)

- Where is...?: Où est...? (oo eh)

- How much is this?: Combien ça coûte? (kohm-byen sah koot)

Directions:

- Left: Gauche (gohsh)

- Right: Droite (dwaht)

- Straight ahead: Tout droit (too dwa)

- Near: Près (preh)

- Far: Loin (lwan)

Dining & Shopping:

- A table for two, please: Une table pour deux, s'il vous plaît (ewn tah-bluh poor duh, seel voo pleh)

- The menu, please: La carte, s'il vous plaît (lah kart, seel voo pleh)

- Check, please: L'addition, s'il vous plaît (lah-dee-syon, seel voo pleh)

- I'm looking for...: Je cherche... (zhuh shersh)

- How much does this cost?: Ça coûte combien? (sah koot kohm-byen)

Emergency Phrases:

- Call the police!: Appelez la police! (ah-peh-lay lah poh-lees)

- I need a doctor: J'ai besoin d'un médecin (zhay buh-zwan dun may-sahn)

- I'm lost: Je suis perdu(e) (zhuh swee pehr-doo)

- Help!: Au secours! (oh suh-koor)

Numbers:

- One: Un (uhn)

- Two: Deux (duh)

- Three: Trois (trwah)

- Ten: Dix (dees)

Chapter 2: The Best Time to Visit Marseille

Marseille is a destination that can be enjoyed throughout the year, offering unique experiences in every season. Whether it's the sun-kissed beaches of summer or the tranquil, charming streets in winter, each season brings something special. Thanks to its Mediterranean climate with hot summers and mild winters, Marseille remains an attractive option no matter when you plan to visit. Here's a look at what each season offers:

Weather in Marseille

Spring (March - May):

Springtime in Marseille is delightful, with temperatures ranging from 12°C to 20°C (54°F to 68°F). It's a great time for outdoor activities since the weather is comfortably warm, and you can avoid the summer crowds. Although there may be the occasional light rain, it's quite rare. The parks and gardens are in full bloom, making it an ideal season for scenic walks and leisurely afternoons in outdoor cafés.

Summer (June - August):

Summer in Marseille is hot, with temperatures ranging from 20°C to 30°C (68°F to 86°F), and sometimes higher during heatwaves. This is the city's busiest time, so expect larger crowds, especially around popular spots like the Calanques and the Old Port. Beaches like Plage des Catalans and Prado Beach are prime attractions during this season. Be ready for busier streets and higher prices, with accommodation costs rising by as much as 50%. It's advisable to book your stay early.

Fall (September - November):

Autumn brings cooler temperatures, ranging between 14°C and 25°C (57°F to 77°F). September and October are particularly pleasant, as the summer crowds begin to thin out, but the sea remains warm enough for a dip. This is also a wonderful time for hiking the Calanques or exploring Marseille's cultural landmarks. Additionally, with fewer tourists around, hotel rates tend to drop, providing better deals than during peak summer.

Winter (December - February):

Winter in Marseille is mild, with daytime temperatures ranging from 5°C to 12°C (41°F to 54°F). Although there's more rain, snow is extremely rare. While it's not beach weather, winter offers a quieter, more authentic side of Marseille, perfect for exploring museums, markets, and restaurants without the hustle of tourists.

Why Visit Marseille in Winter?

Though summer draws the most visitors, winter offers a different and quieter charm to the city. If you prefer fewer crowds and lower prices, winter could be the ideal time for your visit.

Perks of Traveling in Winter:

- **Lower Costs:** Traveling off-season means significant savings on accommodation and flights. You can find hotel rooms up to 40% cheaper than in summer, with mid-range hotels offering rates as low as €60 per night.

- **Cultural Immersion:** With fewer tourists around, winter allows you to experience the local way of life. Wander through vibrant markets like the Marché des Capucins or visit museums and galleries such as the MuCEM (Museum of

European and Mediterranean Civilizations) with ease. Admission to MuCEM is around €11.

- **Winter Cuisine:** Marseille's comforting winter dishes come to life during the colder months. Try hearty meals like cassoulet or daube provençale in cozy restaurants, often without needing a reservation. Many places also offer seasonal menus at lower prices during this time.

- **Christmas Markets & Festivities:** In December, Marseille comes alive with festive cheer, particularly at the Christmas market in the Old Port. These markets feature handmade crafts, Provençal delicacies, and holiday decorations. You'll also find traditional santons—figurines used in Provençal nativity scenes. While entry to the market is free, souvenirs and treats typically range from €5 to €20.

- **Mild Winter Weather:** Even in winter, Marseille's Mediterranean climate allows for outdoor activities. Enjoy a winter hike through the beautiful Calanques or take a peaceful stroll around the Old Port. Daytime temperatures in January often reach 10°C to 12°C (50°F to 54°F),

making it comfortable for sightseeing and
exploring the city.

Chapter 3: Getting to Marseille

Marseille, one of France's most vibrant and historic cities, serves as a central hub for reaching both the Mediterranean coast and the Provence region. Thanks to its well-established transportation links, traveling to Marseille is convenient whether you're arriving by plane, train, bus, car, or even ferry. Here's a guide on how to get to Marseille, with estimated costs and practical tips for each travel option.

Flying to Marseille

Marseille Provence Airport (MRS), located about 25 kilometers (16 miles) from the city center, is the primary airport serving international travelers, making it a convenient entry point for visitors.

International Flights to Marseille

Marseille Provence Airport is well-connected to key European cities and offers some long-haul routes. Major airlines like Air France, Ryanair, EasyJet, Lufthansa, and British Airways operate flights to Marseille. You can fly directly from cities such as:

- London: Around 2 hours

- Paris: 1 hour 20 minutes

- Barcelona: 1 hour 15 minutes

- Rome: 1 hour 30 minutes

- New York: No direct flights; journeys typically take 10-12 hours with connections.

Flight Prices to Marseille

Ticket prices depend on the season, airline, and how far in advance you book. Here are typical price ranges:

- From London: €50 to €150, with budget airlines like Ryanair and EasyJet often offering the cheapest fares.

- From Paris: €50 to €120, with competitive options from Air France and budget carriers.

- From New York: €450 to €900, with layovers.

Tip: Booking 2-3 months ahead can help secure better prices, especially for summer and holiday seasons. Be mindful that budget airlines may charge additional fees for checked baggage and seat selection.

Getting from Marseille Provence Airport to the City Center

Upon arriving at Marseille Provence Airport, you have a few options for getting to the city center:

- **Airport Shuttle Bus (Navette):** Departs every 15 minutes to Gare Saint-Charles, Marseille's main train station. The journey takes about 25 minutes and costs around €10.

- **Taxi:** A taxi ride into the city center ranges from €50 to €70, depending on traffic, and takes 30-40 minutes.

- **Car Rental:** For those planning to explore beyond Marseille, car rentals start at approximately €30 per day.

Getting to Marseille by Train

Traveling by train is a fast and efficient option for those coming from other parts of France or Europe. The French national railway, SNCF, runs regular high-speed trains to Gare Saint-Charles, Marseille's centrally located station.

Trains from Paris to Marseille

The TGV high-speed train is the quickest way to get from Paris to Marseille, with a travel time of around 3 hours 15 minutes. Several departures are available throughout the day.

- **Cost:** Ticket prices range from €45 to €120, depending on how early you book and your choice of travel time.

- **Tip:** To find the best deals, book your tickets in advance or consider Ouigo, a budget-friendly TGV service, with prices starting as low as €25.

Trains from Other European Cities

- **Barcelona:** Direct trains take roughly 4 hours 30 minutes, with fares between €45 and €100.

- **Nice:** The regional TER train takes about 2 hours, with ticket prices ranging from €30 to €50.

- **Milan:** Direct trains take around 7 hours, with fares ranging from €50 to €120.

- **Tip:** Websites like Trainline or SNCF Connect are useful for comparing schedules and prices.

Getting to Marseille by Bus

If you're traveling on a budget or have a flexible schedule, taking a bus is the most affordable way to get to Marseille. Companies like FlixBus, BlaBlaCar Bus, and Eurolines offer routes to Marseille.

Bus from Paris to Marseille

Buses from Paris to Marseille take 9-11 hours, depending on traffic, with tickets priced between €20 and €50.

Bus from Other European Cities

- **Barcelona:** Buses take 7-8 hours, with fares starting at €25.

- **Milan:** The journey takes 8-9 hours, with prices from €30.

- **Nice:** Buses take 2.5-3 hours, costing between €15 and €25.

Though the bus journey is longer, it's a great option for travelers looking to save money.

Driving to Marseille

Driving allows for flexibility, especially if you plan to explore Provence at your own pace. However, parking in Marseille's city center can be challenging, particularly during peak times.

Driving from Paris to Marseille

The drive from Paris to Marseille is around 775 kilometers (482 miles) and takes roughly 7-8 hours, mostly along the A6 and A7 motorways.

- **Costs:** Expect to pay between €60 and €70 for tolls, and €70 to €100 for fuel, depending on your vehicle.

- **Car Rentals:** Daily rental rates start at around €30 to €50 for a basic model.

- **Tip:** Consider parking outside the city center and using public transportation to avoid the hassle of city parking.

Ferries to Marseille

For those traveling by sea, Marseille is connected by ferry to destinations like Corsica, Sardinia, and North Africa (Algeria and Tunisia).

- **Ferry from Corsica:** The journey from Ajaccio to Marseille takes 10-12 hours, with fares ranging from €50 to €120.

- **Ferry from Sardinia:** The ferry from Porto Torres takes approximately 17 hours, with ticket prices starting at €60.

- **Tip:** For longer journeys, booking a cabin can provide extra comfort. Fares can vary, so it's wise to book early, especially during the summer months.

Chapter 4: Where to Stay in Marseille

Marseille offers an array of accommodation options to suit every type of traveler, from luxury enthusiasts to budget-conscious adventurers. Whether you're looking for a hotel with sea views, a stay in the historic center, or a trendy hostel, Marseille has it all. Below is a guide to some of the top hotels, budget options, and the best neighborhoods to stay in during your visit.

Best Hotels in Marseille

1. InterContinental Marseille - Hotel Dieu (5-star)

Located in a majestic 18th-century building overlooking the Vieux-Port, this luxurious hotel offers stunning views of the port and Notre-Dame de la Garde. With its upscale spa and gourmet dining, it's one of the most iconic accommodations in the city.

- **Price:** Rooms from €300, suites starting at €800+ per night
- **Ideal for:** Luxury travelers and couples who prefer a historic and central location.

2. Sofitel Marseille Vieux-Port (5-star)

Situated near the Old Port, this elegant hotel boasts breathtaking views of the harbor from its rooftop terrace. The hotel also offers a spa and fine dining options, and it's within walking distance of major attractions.

- **Price:** Rooms from €250 per night
- **Ideal for:** Travelers seeking luxury near the waterfront and city center.

3. Hôtel La Résidence du Vieux-Port (4-star)

A stylish boutique hotel offering contemporary design with incredible views of the Old Port and Notre-Dame de la Garde. Its central location makes it a great choice for those who want to be in the heart of Marseille.

- **Price:** Rooms from €180 per night
- **Ideal for:** Couples and solo travelers looking for a chic, central stay.

4. Mama Shelter Marseille (3-star)

This quirky, modern hotel is located in the artsy Cours Julien district. With funky designs and affordable rates, it's perfect for those wanting to stay in a lively, creative area.

- **Price:** Rooms from €90 per night

- **Ideal for:** Young travelers and couples looking for a vibrant atmosphere with plenty of street art and nightlife.

Budget Accommodation in Marseille

1. Vertigo Vieux-Port (Hostel)

Located just a short walk from the Old Port, this lively hostel offers both dormitory and private rooms, along with a communal kitchen and bar. It's a fantastic choice for backpackers seeking a social experience.

- **Price:** Dorms from €25, private rooms from €60 per night
- **Ideal for:** Budget travelers and backpackers.

2. Hôtel 96 (3-star)

Set on the outskirts of Marseille, Hôtel 96 provides a peaceful retreat in a serene garden setting. It's an excellent option for travelers looking to escape the city's hustle while still being a short drive from central Marseille.

- **Price:** Rooms from €80 per night
- **Ideal for:** Budget travelers in search of tranquility.

3. Ibis Budget Marseille Vieux-Port (2-star)

For those looking for an affordable and simple stay near the Old Port, this budget hotel offers clean, no-frills accommodations in a prime location.

- **Price:** Rooms from €60 per night
- **Ideal for:** Budget-conscious travelers who prioritize location.

4. The People Hostel – Marseille

Located in the vibrant Panier district, this stylish hostel offers both dormitory and private rooms, as well as an on-site restaurant and rooftop terrace.

- **Price:** Dorm beds from €20, private rooms from €50 per night
- **Ideal for:** Budget travelers and groups who want a stylish yet affordable option.

Luxury Hotels in Marseille

1. Le Petit Nice Passedat (5-star)

Located near the Corniche, this high-end hotel offers stunning sea views and features a Michelin-starred restaurant. With elegant rooms and a swimming pool, it's an ideal choice for a romantic getaway or a special occasion.

- **Price:** Rooms from €500 per night
- **Ideal for:** Food enthusiasts, couples, and anyone seeking an unforgettable experience.

2. C2 Hôtel (5-star)

A boutique hotel in a restored 19th-century mansion, C2 Hôtel combines historic charm with modern luxury. It includes a private spa and is well-positioned for exploring the city.

- **Price:** Rooms from €300 per night
- **Ideal for:** Couples and luxury travelers who appreciate design and tranquility.

3. Nhow Marseille (4-star)

Set along the coastline, Nhow Marseille is a chic and trendy hotel featuring vibrant decor, an infinity pool, and beautiful sea views. Perfect for design-conscious travelers.

- **Price:** Rooms from €250 per night
- **Ideal for:** Couples and design lovers looking for a unique seaside stay.

Best Neighborhoods to Stay in Marseille

1. Vieux-Port (Old Port)

The bustling Old Port is the heart of Marseille. Staying here means being close to markets, restaurants, and top attractions like Notre-Dame de la Garde and the MuCEM.

- **Best for:** First-time visitors, couples, and those wanting to be near the action.
- **Price Range:** Mid-range to luxury (€150 - €300 per night).

2. Le Panier

Le Panier is Marseille's oldest neighborhood, known for its charming narrow streets and colorful buildings. Staying here offers a taste of authentic, historic Marseille.

- **Best for:** History lovers, couples, and solo travelers.
- **Price Range:** Mid-range (€80 - €180 per night).

3. Cours Julien

Famous for its street art and lively cafe scene, Cours Julien is a bohemian neighborhood that attracts young travelers. With its creative energy and nightlife, it's a vibrant area to stay.

- **Best for:** Young travelers, artists, and nightlife enthusiasts.
- **Price Range:** Budget to mid-range (€60 - €150 per night).

4. Prado/La Corniche

For those looking to stay close to the beach, the Prado and La Corniche areas provide a more relaxed environment with seaside promenades and fewer tourists.

- **Best for:** Beach lovers, families, and those seeking a quieter stay.
- **Price Range:** Mid-range to luxury (€100 - €250 per night).

Chapter 5: Top Things to Do in Marseille

Marseille is a vibrant city brimming with history, culture, and natural beauty. Whether you're a history enthusiast, a foodie, or an outdoor lover, there's no shortage of activities to make your visit unforgettable. From ancient fortresses to scenic coastal hikes, here's a guide to some of the city's top experiences, unique spots, and hidden gems.

Best Things to Do in Marseille

1. Basilique Notre-Dame de la Garde

Perched atop the highest point in Marseille, this breathtaking basilica offers intricate mosaics, a golden statue of the Virgin Mary, and panoramic views of the city and sea. It's one of Marseille's most iconic landmarks.

- **Opening Hours:** Daily, 7:00 AM – 6:30 PM (varies by season)
- **Entry Fee:** Free

- **Getting There:** Hike (20-30 minutes), Bus 60, or take the tourist train from the Vieux Port.

2. Vieux Port (Old Port)

The bustling Vieux Port is Marseille's beating heart, where you can see fishermen unloading their catch, stroll along the waterfront, or dine at seafood restaurants. It's also the departure point for boat tours to the Calanques and Château d'If.

- **Opening Hours:** Open 24 hours; restaurants and shops operate throughout the day.
- **Entry Fee:** Free
- **Highlights:** Fresh seafood market, harbor views, street performers.

3. Château d'If

Made famous by *The Count of Monte Cristo*, this 16th-century

island fortress is a captivating visit. Explore the prison cells and take in the views from the ramparts.

- **Opening Hours:** April-September: 10:00 AM – 6:00 PM; October-March: 10:00 AM – 5:00 PM (Closed Mondays).
- **Entry Fee:** €6 adults, free for children under 18.
- **Boat Ride:** €11 round trip from the Vieux Port.

4. MuCEM (Museum of European and Mediterranean Civilizations)

This architectural marvel is located by the Old Port and delves into the history and culture of the Mediterranean. The

modern design and rooftop terrace offer stunning harbor views.

- **Opening Hours:** Wednesday to Monday: 10:00 AM – 7:00 PM; closed Tuesdays.
- **Entry Fee:** €11 full price, €7.50 reduced.
- **Tip:** Free entry on the first Sunday of each month.

Unique Places to Visit in Marseille

1.Les Goudes

A short drive from the city center, this small fishing village offers a rugged coastline, turquoise waters, and an authentic, tranquil atmosphere—ideal for escaping the urban buzz.

- **Best Time to Visit:** Early morning or late afternoon.
- **Entry Fee:** Free
- **What to Do:** Coastal hikes, secluded beaches, fresh seafood at local restaurants.

2. La Vieille Charité

Located in Le Panier district, this 17th-century architectural wonder now houses museums and cultural exhibitions. Its arcaded courtyard and chapel are serene stops during your visit.

- **Opening Hours:** Tuesday to Sunday: 10:00 AM – 6:00 PM.
- **Entry Fee:** Free to enter the courtyard; museum entry costs around €5.
- **Nearby Attractions:** Explore Le Panier, the city's oldest neighborhood.

3. Palais Longchamp

This 19th-century palace houses both the Museum of Fine Arts and the Natural History Museum. Its tranquil gardens and majestic fountains offer an oasis of calm in the city.

- **Opening Hours:** Tuesday to Sunday: 10:00 AM – 6:00 PM; closed Mondays.
- **Entry Fee:** Free to visit the gardens; museum tickets cost €5.
- **What to See:** Grand fountains, art collections, and peaceful gardens.

Free Things to Do in Marseille

1. Wander through Le Panier

Marseille's oldest neighborhood, Le Panier, is full of colorful streets, artisan shops, and vibrant street art. Take a leisurely stroll through its narrow alleys to experience its authentic charm.

- **Opening Hours:** Streets are always open; shops and cafes generally from 10:00 AM – 6:00 PM.
- **Entry Fee:** Free

2. Stroll along the Corniche Kennedy

This coastal road offers stunning views of the Mediterranean, perfect for a leisurely walk or bike ride. Along the way, you'll find beaches, parks, and excellent sunset spots.

- **Opening Hours:** Always open
- **Entry Fee:** Free
- **What to See:** Scenic views, coastal architecture, Monument aux Héros de l'Armée d'Orient.

3. Parc Borély

Escape the hustle and bustle at this sprawling park, complete with gardens, a lake, and plenty of room for picnicking. You can also visit Château Borély, home to the Museum of Decorative Arts, Fashion, and Ceramics.

- **Opening Hours:** Daily, 6:00 AM – 9:00 PM (varies by season).
- **Entry Fee:** Free for the park; museum entry €6.

Must-See Museums in Marseille

1. MuCEM (Museum of European and Mediterranean Civilizations)

A must-visit for its exhibitions, striking architecture, and rooftop views. Its connection to Fort Saint-Jean adds a historic dimension to the experience.

2. Musée des Beaux-Arts

Located in Palais Longchamp, this fine arts museum houses a rich collection of European paintings and sculptures from the 16th to 19th centuries.

- **Opening Hours:** Tuesday to Sunday: 10:00 AM – 6:00 PM.
- **Entry Fee:** €5.

3. Musée d'Histoire de Marseille

This museum near the Vieux Port chronicles Marseille's history, from its Greek origins to the modern day. Exhibits include shipwrecks, ancient artifacts, and multimedia displays.

- **Opening Hours:** Tuesday to Sunday: 10:00 AM – 6:00 PM; closed Mondays.
- **Entry Fee:** €5.

Hidden Gems in Marseille

1. Vallon des Auffes

Just off the Corniche, this picturesque fishing harbor offers brightly colored boats, traditional houses, and a peaceful escape from the city.

- **Best Time to Visit:** Early evening for sunset.

- **Entry Fee:** Free
- **Nearby Eats:** Try Chez Fonfon for bouillabaisse, the iconic fish stew.

2. La Friche la Belle de Mai

This former tobacco factory is now a cultural hub with contemporary art exhibits, rooftop bars, and events like outdoor cinema and concerts.

- **Opening Hours:** Vary by event, but typically open daily.
- **Entry Fee:** Free for outdoor areas; exhibition fees vary.

3. Église Saint-Victor

Dating back to the 5th century, this ancient abbey is a hidden historical treasure. Its atmospheric crypt and commanding view of the Vieux Port make it a fascinating stop.

- **Opening Hours:** Daily, 9:00 AM – 7:00 PM.
- **Entry Fee:** Free
- **Tip:** Don't miss the nearby bakery, famous for its navettes, traditional Marseille biscuits.

Chapter 6: Exploring Marseille's Districts

Marseille is a city of diverse neighborhoods, each brimming with its own unique charm, history, and atmosphere. Whether you're navigating the colorful streets of Le Panier, taking in the sights at the bustling Vieux-Port, or exploring the lively city center, every corner of Marseille has a distinct vibe. Below is a guide to help you discover some of the most iconic and vibrant areas in this fascinating city.

Exploring Le Panier District

Le Panier is Marseille's oldest district, an enchanting blend of narrow streets, historic architecture, and artisan shops. Once the heart of ancient Greek and Roman settlements, today it's a lively, artistic neighborhood that seamlessly marries its rich past with a contemporary, creative spirit.

1. Wander through the Winding Streets

Le Panier is made for wandering. With its maze of cobblestone lanes and charming squares, it's easy to lose yourself in its inviting atmosphere. One of the main streets, **Rue du Panier**, is lined with local cafés, galleries, and boutiques. The area feels like an open-air museum with colorful murals and art at every turn.

- **Tip:** Be sure to wear comfortable shoes since some streets are steep and can be slippery.

2. Visit La Vieille Charité

One of Le Panier's most important landmarks, **La Vieille Charité**, was built in the 17th century as an almshouse. Today, this beautiful complex is home to museums and a cultural center. The central courtyard, lined with arches, offers a peaceful spot to relax.

- **Cost:** Museum entry is €5, but visiting the courtyard is free.

- **Highlight:** Don't miss the **Museum of Mediterranean Archaeology** and the **Museum of African, Oceanic, and Amerindian Arts**.

3. Admire the Street Art

Le Panier is renowned for its vibrant street art, which covers many of the district's buildings. The murals constantly change, making each visit feel new and exciting. If you're a fan of urban art, this district will captivate you.

- **Tip:** Check out the art near **Place des Moulins**, a hot spot for fresh street murals.

4. Enjoy a Coffee at Place de Lenche

Located near the Vieux-Port, **Place de Lenche** is a relaxed square where you can sip a coffee or a glass of wine while enjoying a view of the city below. It's a perfect spot to rest and people-watch after a day of exploring.

- **Cost:** Expect to pay around €3-€5 for a coffee or wine at one of the local cafés.

Visiting Marseille's Vieux-Port

The **Vieux-Port** (Old Port) is the beating heart of Marseille. Once a major trade hub, it's now a lively waterfront district full of cafés, seafood restaurants, and markets. It's also a launching point for boat tours to nearby attractions.

1. Stroll along the Waterfront

A walk along the Vieux-Port is a great way to soak up Marseille's maritime history. The pedestrianized section along the **Quai des Belges** offers stunning views of the harbor and the boats.

- **Cost:** Free to explore.

- **Tip:** Arrive early in the morning to witness the local fish market, where fishermen sell their fresh catch of the day.

2. Take a Boat Tour to Château d'If

A boat trip to **Château d'If** is a must for anyone who loves history. This 16th-century fortress-turned-prison was famously featured in **Alexandre Dumas' *The Count of Monte Cristo***. The short boat ride offers incredible views of Marseille's coastline.

- **Cost:** Boat trips start at around €10, and entry to the Château is €6.

- **Tip:** Boats leave regularly from the Vieux-Port throughout the day.

3. Discover the MuCEM

The **Museum of European and Mediterranean Civilizations (MuCEM)** is a striking modern structure located at the mouth of the Old Port. Inside, you'll find fascinating exhibitions about Mediterranean culture and history, along with sweeping views from its rooftop terrace.

- **Cost:** €11 per adult; free on the first Sunday of every month.

- **Tip:** The views from the museum's rooftop are among the best in Marseille.

4. Ride the Ferris Wheel

For panoramic views of Marseille and the Mediterranean, take a ride on the **Ferris wheel** near the Vieux-Port. This family-friendly attraction offers incredible vistas, especially at sunset.

- **Cost:** Around €5 per person.

- **Tip:** Sunset rides provide the best photo opportunities.

5. Explore Fort Saint-Jean

Fort Saint-Jean, built in the 17th century, stands at the entrance to the Vieux-Port. Now part of the MuCEM complex, it's a wonderful place to explore with free entry to its gardens and scenic paths.

- **Cost:** Free to enter.

- **Tip:** The fort's elevated gardens are a peaceful escape with unbeatable views of the Mediterranean.

Marseille City Center: Highlights

Marseille's city center is an energetic mix of historic landmarks and modern life. From grand avenues to lively markets, it's a must-visit area that reflects the dynamic pulse of the city.

1. La Canebière

This is Marseille's main boulevard, running from the Vieux-Port up to the **Réformés quarter**. Lined with shops, historic buildings, and cafés, **La Canebière** was once the city's most prestigious street.

- **Cost:** Free to explore.

- **Tip:** Stop for a coffee break at one of the many cafés along the street.

2. Palais Longchamp

The 19th-century **Palais Longchamp** houses the **Musée des Beaux-Arts** and the **Natural History Museum**. The palace is surrounded by beautifully landscaped gardens and fountains, perfect for a quiet afternoon.

- **Cost:** Entry to the museums is around €6, but the gardens are free.

- **Tip:** The fountains are a serene place to unwind after a day of sightseeing.

3. Cours Julien

This bohemian quarter is known for its eclectic street art, hip cafés, and lively atmosphere. **Cours Julien** is popular with artists and musicians, and its nightlife scene comes alive after dark.

- **Cost:** Free to explore; meals at local spots start from €10-€15.

- **Tip:** Visit on Thursdays to catch the local farmers' market.

4. Noailles Market

For a true taste of Marseille's multicultural side, visit **Noailles Market**, just off **La Canebière**. The vibrant market reflects the city's North African and Mediterranean influences, offering fresh produce, spices, and street food.

- **Cost:** Free to explore; snacks from vendors start at around €2.

- **Tip:** Visit in the morning for the best selection of fresh goods.

5. Opéra de Marseille

The **Opéra de Marseille**, located near the Vieux-Port, is a cultural gem. Whether attending a performance or simply admiring its architecture, it's an iconic stop in the city center.

- **Cost:** Tickets range from €15 to €100, depending on the performance.

- **Tip:** Be sure to check the schedule in advance, as tickets for popular shows sell out quickly.

Chapter 7: Day Trips from Marseille

Marseille's prime location along the Mediterranean coast makes it an excellent base for exploring the broader Provence region and beyond. From charming seaside towns to natural wonders and historic villages, the options for day trips are plentiful. Here's your guide to some top day trips, including scenic getaways to Provence, Cassis, and the breathtaking Calanques National Park.

Day Trips from Marseille to Provence

Provence is a region steeped in history and beauty, famous for its lavender fields, quaint towns, and sun-soaked countryside. A day trip from Marseille can take you through some of the most picturesque landscapes in France.

1. Aix-en-Provence

Just 30 minutes from Marseille, Aix-en-Provence is a sophisticated town known for its elegant squares, lively markets, and fountains. Stroll down the famous Cours Mirabeau, visit the Musée Granet, and enjoy the charming atmosphere of this Provençal gem.

- **Getting There**: Regular trains and buses run between Marseille and Aix; tickets cost around €8-€15 one way.

- **Must-See**: Don't miss the impressive Saint-Sauveur Cathedral and the famous artist Cézanne's studio.

2. Avignon

Avignon offers a step back into medieval times, with its majestic Palais des Papes and the iconic Pont d'Avignon. This UNESCO-listed city is also known for its annual cultural festival, held each summer.

- **Getting There**: Trains from Marseille to Avignon take about 1 hour; tickets range from €15-€30.

- **Must-See**: The Palais des Papes is one of the largest Gothic palaces in Europe and an absolute must-see.

3. Les Baux-de-Provence and Arles

For history buffs, a visit to Les Baux-de-Provence and Arles is a must. Les Baux is a dramatic hilltop village, offering stunning views and ancient ruins, while Arles is famed for its Roman amphitheater and connection to Vincent van Gogh.

- **Getting There**: The most convenient way to visit both is by car, about 1.5 hours from Marseille.

- **Must-See**: The Roman amphitheater in Arles and Château des Baux are the highlights.

Day Trip to Cassis from Marseille

Cassis, located just 30 minutes from Marseille, is a charming fishing village nestled between steep cliffs and the Mediterranean Sea. It offers a perfect day trip with its idyllic harbor, colorful streets, and the nearby Calanques.

1. Explore the Harbor and Town

The picturesque harbor is the heart of Cassis, lined with cafes and restaurants that serve fresh seafood. Stroll through the narrow streets to discover small shops selling local wines, olive oil, and crafts.

- **Getting There**: Trains and buses regularly run from Marseille to Cassis, with train tickets starting at around €5. A drive or taxi takes about 30-40 minutes.

- **Tip**: Arrive early if driving, as parking in Cassis is limited.

2. Visit Cap Canaille

Cap Canaille is one of Europe's highest sea cliffs, offering breathtaking views over the Mediterranean coastline. Whether you choose to drive or hike, the stunning vistas are well worth the effort.

- **Cost**: Free.

- **Tip**: Sunset is the best time to visit for unforgettable views.

3. Wine Tasting in the Vineyards

Cassis is renowned for its white wines, particularly made from Marsanne and Clairette grapes. Several vineyards around the town offer tours and tastings.

- **Cost**: Tastings typically start at €10-€15 per person.

- **Tip**: Visit Domaine du Paternel or Clos Sainte Magdeleine, two of the region's top vineyards.

Visiting Calanques National Park

The Calanques National Park is a natural wonder, with its striking limestone cliffs plunging into turquoise waters. Whether you're a hiker, swimmer, or kayaker, the

Calanques offer an unforgettable escape into nature, just minutes from Marseille.

1. Hiking the Calanques

Hiking is the best way to explore the Calanques. Trails of varying difficulty lead to hidden coves and offer dramatic views of the Mediterranean. Popular Calanques include Sormiou, Morgiou, and the remote yet beautiful En-Vau.

- **Cost**: Free to hike.

- **Tip**: Bring plenty of water and sturdy shoes. Some trails may close in the summer due to fire risks, so check ahead.

2. Swimming and Sunbathing

Many Calanques feature small, secluded beaches perfect for swimming and sunbathing. The clear waters of Calanque d'En-Vau are especially popular, but it requires a bit of hiking to access.

- **Cost**: Free.

- **Tip**: The beaches are rocky, so bring water shoes for more comfortable swimming.

3. Kayaking and Boat Tours

If hiking sounds too strenuous, exploring the Calanques by kayak or boat is a great alternative. Kayaks can take you into hidden coves, while boat tours offer a more relaxed way to see the dramatic cliffs and sparkling waters.

- **Cost**: Kayak rentals start at €20-€40 for a half-day. Boat tours from Marseille or Cassis cost around €25-€35 per person.

- **Tip**: Book in advance, especially in the summer, as kayaking tours fill up quickly.

How to Visit Calanques from Marseille

There are several ways to access the Calanques from Marseille, depending on whether you prefer to hike, boat, or kayak.

1. By Public Transport and Hiking

Public buses from Marseille can take you to trailheads for hiking. Bus 23 to Luminy connects to trails for Calanque de Sormiou and Morgiou, while Bus 21 to Les Baumettes is the starting point for Calanque de Sugiton.

- **Cost**: Bus tickets are about €2 each way.

- **Tip**: Start early to avoid the midday heat.

2. By Boat Tour

Boat tours from Marseille's Vieux-Port provide a scenic way to see the Calanques. The tours last 2-4 hours and offer great views of the cliffs and coves.

- **Cost**: Around €25 per person.

- **Tip**: Booking in advance is essential during summer.

3. By Car and Hiking

Driving allows more flexibility, but parking is limited, especially in summer. You can drive to parking areas near the Calanques, such as Sormiou or Morgiou, and hike from there.

- **Cost**: Parking fees range from €5-€10.

- **Tip**: Arrive early to secure a spot.

Chapter 8: Marseille Tours and Activities

Exploring Marseille's rich history, diverse culture, and stunning landscapes is an adventure best experienced through various tours and activities. From walking through historic districts to cruising the Mediterranean coastline, Marseille offers an array of experiences for history buffs, foodies, outdoor enthusiasts, and art lovers alike. Here's a comprehensive guide to some of the best tours and activities, including walking, biking, wine tours, and boat excursions.

Walking Tours in Marseille

Walking tours are an excellent way to get up close to Marseille's historic neighborhoods, explore its lively street art scene, and discover hidden gems. Whether you're new to the city or a frequent visitor, these tours give you an insider's view of Marseille's charm.

1. Le Panier Walking Tour

- Explore the oldest district of Marseille, **Le Panier**, filled with winding streets, vibrant street art, and historic landmarks like **La Vieille Charité**.
- **Duration**: 2-3 hours

- **Cost**: €15-€30 per person
- **Highlight**: Discover hidden courtyards and learn about Marseille's multicultural past in this fascinating neighborhood.

2. Vieux-Port Walking Tour

- The **Vieux-Port** is the heart of the city. A guided tour takes you through its bustling maritime history, from the local fish market at **Quai des Belges** to the panoramic views from **Fort Saint-Jean** and the **MuCEM**.
- **Duration**: 1.5-2 hours
- **Cost**: €10-€25 per person
- **Highlight**: The fish market and panoramic views over the harbor from Fort Saint-Jean.

Bike Tours in Marseille

For those who prefer to explore on two wheels, bike tours offer a fun and eco-friendly way to cover more ground. Marseille's diverse terrain, from coastal roads to hilly neighborhoods, makes for exciting cycling routes.

1. Marseille City Bike Tour

- Ride through the city center, visiting key landmarks like **Palais Longchamp**, the **Corniche**, and **Notre-Dame de la Garde**.
- **Duration**: 3-4 hours
- **Cost**: €35-€45 per person (including bike rental)
- **Highlight**: Cycling along the Corniche with stunning views of the Mediterranean.

2. Electric Bike Tour to Notre-Dame de la Garde

- Perfect for those who want to tackle Marseille's hills with ease, this electric bike tour takes you to the top of **Notre-Dame de la Garde** for unbeatable panoramic views.
- **Duration**: 2-3 hours
- **Cost**: €40-€50 per person (including electric bike rental)
- **Highlight**: Sweeping views of Marseille from the basilica, without the effort of traditional cycling.

Boat Tours in Marseille

With its scenic coastline, a boat tour is a must-do in Marseille. Whether you're visiting the **Calanques**, exploring nearby islands, or just enjoying the view from the water, there's a tour for everyone.

1. Calanques Boat Tour

- Sail along the jagged coastline of **Calanques National Park** and admire the limestone cliffs and hidden coves. Some tours also allow time for swimming and snorkeling in the clear waters.
- **Duration**: 3-4 hours
- **Cost**: €25-€35 per person
- **Highlight**: Seeing the stunning **Calanque d'En-Vau** from the water and swimming in the crystal-clear Mediterranean.

2. Château d'If and Frioul Islands Boat Tour

- A boat trip from **Vieux-Port** to the **Château d'If**, famous from *The Count of Monte Cristo*, followed by a visit to the nearby **Frioul Islands** for hiking and beach time.
- **Duration**: 2-3 hours
- **Cost**: €15-€20 for the boat ride, plus €6 entry to Château d'If
- **Highlight**: Exploring the historic fortress and the peaceful, rugged beauty of the Frioul Islands.

Wine Tours in Marseille

Marseille is located near Provence's renowned wine regions, making it an ideal base for wine-tasting excursions. From the crisp whites of Cassis to the famous rosés of Provence, wine lovers will find plenty to enjoy.

1. Cassis Wine Tour

- Visit the vineyards surrounding **Cassis**, a short drive from Marseille, and sample the area's famed white wines. The tour includes tastings at renowned vineyards.
- **Duration**: 4-5 hours
- **Cost**: €60-€90 per person
- **Highlight**: Tastings at prestigious vineyards like **Clos Sainte Magdeleine** or **Domaine du Paternel**.

2. Provence Wine Tour

- Explore several vineyards in the broader **Provence** wine region, sampling red, white, and rosé wines. A full-day tour includes visits to multiple estates.
- **Duration**: Full day
- **Cost**: €90-€150 per person

- **Highlight**: Tasting a variety of wines, particularly the region's famed rosé.

Street Art Tours in Marseille

Marseille boasts a vibrant street art scene, with bold murals and graffiti adorning the walls of neighborhoods like **Cours Julien** and **Le Panier**. Discover the city's creative side with a street art tour.

1. Cours Julien Street Art Tour

- Wander through the colorful streets of **Cours Julien**, a hub for street artists, and see the most impressive murals and graffiti while learning about the artists and their works.
- **Duration**: 2-3 hours
- **Cost**: €20-€30 per person
- **Highlight**: The bohemian vibe of **Cours Julien**, where the art is constantly evolving.

2. Le Panier Street Art and History Tour

- Combine history and street art on a tour of **Le Panier**, exploring both the district's ancient architecture and its thriving street art scene.
- **Duration**: 2-3 hours
- **Cost**: €25-€35 per person

- **Highlight**: The striking contrast between the historic streets and the modern murals.

Historical Walking Tours in Marseille

Dive deep into Marseille's long and storied past with a historical walking tour. From ancient Greek and Roman ruins to key sites from the French Revolution and World War II, history lovers will find plenty to fascinate them.

1. Ancient Marseille Walking Tour

- Visit key archaeological sites like the **Roman Docks** and the **Jardin des Vestiges** while learning about the city's origins as a Greek colony and its evolution over the centuries.
- **Duration**: 2-3 hours
- **Cost**: €15-€25 per person
- **Highlight**: Touring the ancient ruins and getting a glimpse of Marseille's earliest days.

2. Revolutionary and WWII History Tour

- Learn about Marseille's role in both the French Revolution and World War II, visiting sites such as the **Hôtel de Ville** and **Fort Saint-Nicolas**.
- **Duration**: 2 hours
- **Cost**: €20 per person

- **Highlight**: Discovering Marseille's rich history of resistance and revolution.

Marseille Hop-on Hop-off Bus Tour

For those who prefer to explore at their own pace, the **hop-on hop-off bus tour** is a convenient option. With stops at all of Marseille's main attractions, from **Notre-Dame de la Garde** to the **MuCEM**, this tour lets you explore the city's highlights while providing informative commentary.

- **Duration**: Tickets valid for 24 or 48 hours

- **Cost**: €20-€25 per adult

- **Highlight**: Flexibility to explore at your own pace with easy access to Marseille's major sights.

Chapter 9: Marseille's Culinary Scene

Marseille's vibrant culinary landscape is a delicious reflection of its Mediterranean location and rich cultural history. Known for fresh seafood, Provençal flavors, and international influences, the city offers something for every taste. From fine dining establishments to local food markets and street stalls, Marseille's dining scene is a feast for the senses. Whether you're a foodie or simply curious to explore local flavors, this guide to Marseille's best restaurants, cafes, and food tours will ensure you get a true taste of the city.

Best Restaurants in Marseille

Marseille offers a range of dining experiences, from Michelin-starred fine dining to cozy bistros serving traditional Provençal cuisine. Here are some standout options for any culinary adventure:

1. Le Petit Nice – Passedat

A three-Michelin-starred restaurant, Le Petit Nice is celebrated for its refined and innovative seafood dishes. Perched by the Mediterranean, it offers breathtaking views alongside an elegant dining experience. Chef Gérald

Passedat crafts each dish with local, fresh ingredients, elevating traditional Marseille flavors.

- **Price**: €250-€300 per person for the tasting menu.
- **Highlight**: The "Bouille Abaisse" menu, a modern take on Marseille's iconic bouillabaisse.

2. AM par Alexandre Mazzia

At AM, Chef Alexandre Mazzia redefines Mediterranean cuisine with his inventive and artful dishes. Known for pushing culinary boundaries, the Michelin-starred restaurant offers an intimate and creative dining experience.

- **Price**: €150-€250 per person for a tasting menu.
- **Highlight**: A surprise tasting menu that fuses Mediterranean flavors with global influences.

3. Chez Fonfon

For an authentic taste of Marseille, Chez Fonfon is the place to go. Located in the charming Vallon des Auffes, this historic restaurant is best known for its bouillabaisse, served in the traditional style with a variety of local fish.

- **Price**: Bouillabaisse starts at €60-€70 per person.

- **Highlight**: Classic bouillabaisse, prepared in the Marseille tradition.

Best Cafes in Marseille

Marseille's cafe scene is a mix of cozy spots for a relaxing coffee break and lively venues perfect for people-watching or enjoying a quick snack. Here are a few must-visit cafes:

1. La Fiancée

Trendy and laid-back, La Fiancée is known for its specialty coffee and light brunch offerings. With minimalist décor and a welcoming vibe, it's the perfect spot to start your day or unwind in the afternoon.

- **Price**: Coffee and pastries around €3-€5; brunch options start at €10.
- **Highlight**: Their avocado toast and homemade cakes.

2. Café de l'Abbaye

This popular café near the Old Port offers a perfect combination of great coffee, a laid-back atmosphere, and beautiful views of the harbor. It's especially popular at sunset, making it ideal for a leisurely drink.

- **Price**: Coffee around €2-€3; small plates from €5.

- **Highlight**: The stunning view of the Vieux-Port while sipping your favorite drink.

3. Les Arcenaulx

Combining a café, brasserie, and bookstore, Les Arcenaulx is a unique cultural spot where you can enjoy a coffee or a meal while surrounded by books and art.

- **Price**: Coffee and dessert from €5-€10; main dishes around €20.
- **Highlight**: A charming ambiance with a menu that merges cuisine and culture.

Local Cuisine of Marseille

Marseille's culinary traditions are deeply rooted in its Mediterranean location, with a strong emphasis on seafood, olive oil, and vibrant flavors. Some iconic dishes to try include:

1. Bouillabaisse

This world-famous Provençal fish stew is Marseille's signature dish, made with a variety of local fish and served with rouille (garlic mayonnaise) and crusty bread.

- **Where to try**: Chez Fonfon, L'Epuisette.
- **Price**: €60-€80 per person.

2. Panisse

A popular Marseille snack, panisse is made from chickpea flour and fried or baked to perfection. Crispy on the outside and soft inside, it's a delightful appetizer.

- **Where to try**: Les Panisses du Cours Julien.
- **Price**: €5-€10 for a serving.

3. Aioli

A quintessential Provençal dish, "Le Grand Aioli" features garlic aioli sauce served with boiled vegetables, fish, and seafood. It's a Marseille specialty, perfect for sharing.

- **Where to try**: La Boîte à Sardine, Chez Madie Les Galinettes.
- **Price**: €15-€25 per plate.

Best Seafood in Marseille

As a port city, Marseille is famous for its incredibly fresh seafood. Whether you're looking for a high-end experience or something more casual, here are the top seafood spots:

1. L'Epuisette

Overlooking the Mediterranean, this Michelin-starred restaurant offers an upscale seafood dining experience.

Expect beautifully presented dishes featuring local fish and shellfish.

- **Price**: €120-€150 per person.
- **Highlight**: Fresh oysters and langoustines.

2. La Boîte à Sardine

A laid-back seafood restaurant, La Boîte à Sardine is beloved for its no-frills approach to serving the freshest catch of the day.

- **Price**: Main dishes from €15-€30.
- **Highlight**: Daily specials like sardines and mackerel.

3. Toinou

Offering a casual, self-service seafood experience, Toinou is perfect for enjoying high-quality seafood on a budget. Choose from an array of shellfish and freshly grilled fish.

- **Price**: Oysters from €12 a dozen; main dishes €15-€25.
- **Highlight**: Affordable shellfish platters.

Romantic Restaurants in Marseille

Marseille's scenic waterfront and historic streets provide a perfect setting for a romantic dinner. For a special occasion, these restaurants offer unforgettable dining experiences:

1. Le Rowing Club

With its rooftop terrace overlooking the Vieux-Port, Le Rowing Club is an ideal spot for a romantic meal. The Mediterranean-inspired menu adds to the ambiance.

- **Price**: Main courses from €25-€35.
- **Highlight**: Sunset views from the terrace.

2. L'Epuisette

A favorite for couples, L'Epuisette's intimate setting and exceptional seafood make it one of Marseille's most romantic restaurants.

- **Price**: €120-€150 per person.
- **Highlight**: Seaside dining with stunning Mediterranean views.

3. Peron

Perched on the cliffs overlooking the sea, Peron offers dramatic coastal views and a menu of fresh, Mediterranean dishes.

- **Price**: €70-€100 per person.

- **Highlight**: Savoring fresh oysters with a panoramic view of the sunset.

Cheap Eats in Marseille

Dining in Marseille doesn't have to be expensive. The city is full of affordable eateries serving delicious, authentic meals:

1. La Cantinetta

Located in the Cours Julien area, this cozy spot offers generous portions of Italian-inspired Mediterranean dishes at reasonable prices.

- **Price**: Pizzas and pastas €10-€15.
- **Highlight**: Homemade fresh pasta.

2. Chez Etienne

Famous for its simple yet delicious wood-fired pizzas, Chez Etienne is a favorite among locals for its relaxed vibe and tasty pizzas.

- **Price**: Pizzas €10-€12.
- **Highlight**: Thin-crust pizzas with local toppings.

3. L'Inattendu

A hidden gem in Noailles, L'Inattendu serves hearty Mediterranean dishes influenced by North African flavors.

- **Price**: Main dishes €8-€15.
- **Highlight**: Flavorful couscous and tagines.

Food Tours in Marseille

If you're looking to explore Marseille's culinary diversity, food tours offer a fantastic way to taste local specialties while learning about the city's food culture:

1. Marseille Food Walking Tour

This guided walking tour takes you through the city's most vibrant neighborhoods, with stops to sample local treats such as navettes, Provençal olives, and fresh seafood.

- **Duration**: 3-4 hours.
- **Cost**: €70-€90 per person.
- **Highlight**: Tasting stops at artisanal shops and local markets.

2. Provençal Cooking Class and Market Tour

Combine a hands-on cooking experience with a visit to one of Marseille's lively food markets. You'll learn to prepare a traditional Provençal meal and enjoy it in a relaxed setting.

- **Duration**: 4-5 hours.
- **Cost**: €100-€150 per person.
- **Highlight**: Cooking and dining in a local chef's home.

Chapter 10: Marseille's Nightlife and Entertainment

Marseille's nightlife is a blend of chic rooftop bars, lively clubs, and intimate venues, making it an ideal destination for any night out. Whether you're looking for cocktails with a view, a vibrant club scene, or a romantic evening, Marseille offers a variety of options for every taste. Here's a guide to the best spots for enjoying the city's nightlife after dark.

Best Rooftop Bars in Marseille

Rooftop bars in Marseille provide stunning vistas of the Mediterranean Sea, historic landmarks, and the surrounding mountains. They're perfect for sipping a sunset cocktail or enjoying an evening under the stars.

1. Rooftop R2 – Les Terrasses du Port: Located atop the **Terrasses du Port** shopping center, **Rooftop R2** is one of the city's most popular rooftop bars. Its panoramic views over the Mediterranean and bustling port make it a go-to spot for sunset cocktails and DJ sets.

- **Signature Drinks**: Classic cocktails and local wines.
- **Prices**: Cocktails €12-€15; beers €6-€8.

- **Best Time to Visit**: Arrive early to catch the sunset (around 7-8 PM in summer).

2. Sofitel Marseille Vieux-Port – Dantès Skylounge

For a more upscale rooftop experience, visit **Dantès Skylounge** at the **Sofitel Marseille Vieux-Port**. This elegant bar offers breathtaking views of the Old Port and **Basilique Notre-Dame de la Garde**, perfect for a romantic night out.

- **Signature Drinks**: Try the "Dantès Dream" or a glass of champagne.
- **Prices**: Cocktails €15-€20.
- **Best Time to Visit**: Arrive just before sunset for the best ambiance.

3. Le Rooftop by Radisson Blu: Overlooking the Old Port, **Le Rooftop** at the **Radisson Blu Hotel** offers a casual yet chic atmosphere. With cozy seating, lounge music, and a diverse crowd, it's a great spot to relax and enjoy the city views.

- **Signature Drinks**: From mojitos to martinis.
- **Prices**: Cocktails €12-€14.
- **Best Time to Visit**: Between 8-11 PM for an evening drink.

Marseille Nightlife Guide

From laid-back bars to pulsating nightclubs, Marseille's nightlife is as varied as its population. Whether you're seeking a relaxed evening or a party that lasts until dawn, the city's diverse venues have something for everyone.

1. La Friche La Belle de Mai: A former tobacco factory turned cultural hub, **La Friche La Belle de Mai** is a favorite for locals. By day, it hosts art exhibits, and by night, it transforms into a vibrant open-air venue for music events.

- **Music Style**: Electronic, house, indie.
- **Vibe**: Artsy and laid-back.
- **Prices**: Entry €5-€15, beers €5, cocktails €10.
- **Best Nights**: Fridays and Saturdays, especially in summer.

2. Cours Julien: Known for its bohemian vibe, **Cours Julien** is filled with street art, trendy bars, and cozy cafés. Popular spots like **La Caravelle** and **Oogie** offer live music, craft beers, and a multicultural crowd.

- **Music Style**: Jazz, indie rock, DJ sets.
- **Vibe**: Artsy, relaxed.
- **Prices**: Beers €6-€8, cocktails €10-€12.

- **Best Nights**: Thursday to Saturday.

3. Le Trolleybus: A Marseille nightlife institution, **Le Trolleybus** offers multiple rooms with different music genres, from electronic to disco. Located near the Old Port, it's a must-visit for anyone looking to dance the night away.

- **Music Style**: House, electro, pop, 80s hits.
- **Vibe**: Lively and energetic.
- **Prices**: Entry €10-€15, drinks €8-€12.
- **Best Nights**: Friday and Saturday, 11 PM to 5 AM.

4. L'Intermédiaire: For live music in a more intimate setting, head to **L'Intermédiaire** in the **La Plaine** district. This venue hosts live bands, open mic nights, and local DJ sets, attracting students and music lovers alike.

- **Music Style**: Rock, indie, funk, acoustic.
- **Vibe**: Casual and friendly.
- **Prices**: Beers €5, cocktails €8.
- **Best Nights**: Thursdays for live music, weekends for DJ sets.

Romantic Nightlife Experiences in Marseille

For couples, Marseille offers a range of romantic nightlife options, from scenic boat cruises to intimate bars with live jazz. These are perfect for a special evening with your partner.

1. **Sunset Cruise Along the Mediterranean**: A sunset cruise along Marseille's stunning coastline is an unforgettable romantic experience. Tours depart from the Old Port and sail past the **Frioul Islands** and the **Calanques**.

- **Price**: €25-€50 per person, depending on the provider.
- **Duration**: 2-3 hours.
- **Best Time to Visit**: Around 7 PM in summer for optimal sunset views.

2. **Dinner at Le Petit Nice Passedat**: For an upscale romantic dinner, **Le Petit Nice Passedat**, a Michelin-starred restaurant, is an exquisite choice. Located by the sea, the restaurant specializes in gourmet Mediterranean cuisine.

- **Menu**: Opt for a tasting menu to experience the chef's finest dishes.
- **Prices**: €150-€250 per person, including wine pairings.
- **Best Time to Visit**: Book a table for dinner to enjoy sunset views over the Mediterranean.

2. Romantic Stroll along the Corniche: Take a peaceful walk along the **Corniche Kennedy**, a scenic coastal promenade with stunning views of the Mediterranean. Whether at sunset or under the stars, it's a quiet, intimate way to end the evening.

- **Vibe**: Scenic and serene.
- **Cost**: Free.
- **Best Time to Visit**: Just before sunset or in the evening for the twinkling city lights.

3. Drinks at La Caravelle: For a cozy and intimate evening, head to **La Caravelle**, a vintage-style bar near the Old Port. With live jazz music and a romantic ambiance, it's perfect for an evening drink with a loved one.

- **Signature Drinks**: Local **Pastis** or a classic cocktail.
- **Prices**: €7-€12 per drink.

- **Best Time to Visit**: Evenings for live music and a relaxed atmosphere.

Chapter 11: Shopping in Marseille

Marseille offers a diverse and vibrant shopping experience, from high-end malls and boutique stores to bustling street markets and artisanal crafts. Whether you're in search of designer fashion, unique souvenirs, or local products like soap and Provençal goods, the city is a treasure trove for all types of shoppers.

Shopping Malls in Marseille

For a modern shopping experience, Marseille has several large malls that feature everything from international brands to local designers.

1. Les Terrasses du Port

Overlooking the Mediterranean, Les Terrasses du Port is one of Marseille's largest malls, featuring over 190 stores and a stunning rooftop terrace with sea views.

- **Stores:** Zara, Sephora, Apple Store, and more.
- **Dining:** Numerous cafés and restaurants, with a terrace offering panoramic sea views.
- **Hours:** Open daily from 10:00 am to 8:00 pm (restaurants stay open later).
- **Highlight:** Rooftop terrace with breathtaking views of the Mediterranean.

- **Getting there:** Tram T2 or Bus 82S.

2. Centre Bourse

Located near the Vieux-Port, Centre Bourse is a favorite shopping destination for locals and tourists alike. It's also home to the **Musée d'Histoire de Marseille**.

- **Stores:** Fnac, Galeries Lafayette, H&M, and others.
- **Dining:** Cafés and fast food inside the mall.
- **Hours:** Open Monday to Saturday from 10:00 am to 7:30 pm.
- **Highlight:** Proximity to historical sites like the Vieux-Port.
- **Getting there:** Short walk from the Vieux-Port metro station (Line 1).

3. Prado Shopping

A more upscale shopping center, Prado Shopping is located near Stade Vélodrome, offering a luxurious experience with trendy boutiques and high-end brands.

- **Stores:** Nike, Lacoste, Adidas, and more.
- **Dining:** Various cafés and gourmet food spots.
- **Hours:** Open Monday to Saturday from 9:30 am to 8:00 pm.

- **Highlight:** Elegant design and premium shopping experience.
- **Getting there:** Metro Line 2, Rond-Point du Prado station.

Local Souvenirs in Marseille

No trip to Marseille is complete without picking up a few iconic souvenirs. From traditional soaps to artisanal crafts, here are some must-buy items:

1. Savon de Marseille

The quintessential Marseille souvenir, this traditional soap is made from olive oil and has been a staple of Provençal households for centuries.

- **Where to buy:** La Grande Savonnerie, Savonnerie du Midi, or Le Serail.
- **Price:** €4-€8 per bar.
- **Highlight:** Look for the signature "72% olive oil" stamp on the iconic cube-shaped bars.

2. Provençal Lavender Products

Lavender is synonymous with Provence, and you'll find it in everything from essential oils to soaps and sachets.

- **Where to buy:** Marché de Noailles, specialty shops.
- **Price:** €3-€5 for sachets, €10-€20 for essential oils.

3. Pastis

This anise-flavored spirit is a popular local drink, perfect as a souvenir for those wanting a taste of Provence at home.

- **Where to buy:** Maison du Pastis or supermarkets.
- **Price:** €15-€30 per bottle.
- **Highlight:** Ricard and Pernod are the most famous brands.

4. Provençal Ceramics

These hand-painted ceramics, featuring the bright colors of Provence, make excellent gifts or decorative pieces.

- **Where to buy:** Le Panier district, local markets.
- **Price:** €10-€30 depending on the item.

5. Local Food Products

Take home a taste of Provence with local olive oil, herbes de Provence, tapenade, or a bottle of regional rosé.

- **Where to buy:** Les Halles de la Major, epiceries, and markets.
- **Price:** Olive oil starts at €6; wines from €8-€30.

Street Markets in Marseille

For a more authentic and vibrant shopping experience, Marseille's street markets are a must-visit. From fresh produce to local crafts, here are the top markets to explore:

1. Marché de Noailles

One of Marseille's oldest markets, located in the multicultural Noailles district, offering fresh fruits, vegetables, and exotic spices.

- **When to visit:** Daily (except Sundays) from 8:00 am to 1:00 pm.
- **Highlight:** Vibrant atmosphere and wide selection of ethnic foods.

2. Marché du Prado

Stretching along Boulevard du Prado, this large market offers everything from clothing to household goods and local foods.

- **When to visit:** Monday to Saturday from 8:00 am to 1:00 pm.
- **Highlight:** The sheer size and variety make it perfect for bargain hunting.

3. Marché des Capucins

Located in the heart of Noailles, this market is a food lover's paradise with fresh seafood, fruits, vegetables, and Mediterranean specialties.

- **When to visit:** Daily (except Sunday) from 7:30 am to 1:00 pm.
- **Highlight:** North African ingredients and spices, offering a rich culinary experience.

4. Le Panier Artisanal Markets

Explore the charming streets of Le Panier, where artisanal markets offer handmade crafts, jewelry, and art.

- **When to visit:** Weekends or during special events.
- **Highlight:** Unique handcrafted souvenirs and the opportunity to meet local artisans.

5. Les Puces de Fifi (Flea Market)

This quirky flea market in the Cours Julien neighborhood is perfect for discovering vintage treasures, antiques, and retro clothing.

- **When to visit:** Sundays from 8:00 am to 1:00 pm.
- **Highlight:** The artistic vibe of Cours Julien and eclectic finds.

Chapter 12: Outdoor Activities and Nature in Marseille

Marseille is a paradise for outdoor lovers, with its stunning landscapes, Mediterranean coastline, and natural surroundings. Whether you enjoy hiking rugged cliffs, swimming in turquoise waters, or simply relaxing in a park, Marseille offers a multitude of ways to experience nature.

Hiking Near Marseille

The rugged terrain around Marseille offers a diverse range of hiking opportunities, from coastal paths with breathtaking views to serene forested trails. Here's where to explore:

1. Calanques National Park:

The crown jewel of Marseille's natural attractions, Calanques National Park, offers stunning hiking routes that weave through limestone cliffs and hidden coves. The park is a haven for those seeking dramatic scenery and tranquil beaches.

- **Trail difficulty:** Moderate to challenging.

- **Highlights:** Spectacular cliffs, secluded coves, and clear blue waters.

- **Popular route:** The Cassis to Calanque d'En-Vau trail offers one of the park's most scenic hikes.

- **Tip:** Pack plenty of water and sunscreen, as the trails offer little shade.

- **Cost:** Free.

2. Mont Puget:

For seasoned hikers, Mont Puget offers a challenging climb with sweeping views of Marseille, the Calanques, and the Mediterranean.

- **Trail difficulty:** Challenging.

- **Highlights:** Panoramic views of the city and surrounding areas.

- **Starting point:** Luminy, accessible by public transport (Bus 21).

- **Duration:** 5-6 hours round trip.

- **Cost:** Free.

3. Garlaban Massif:

The Garlaban Massif, located just outside the city, offers a variety of hikes through landscapes made famous by the writer Marcel Pagnol. The trails meander through hills and valleys, offering incredible views over Provence.

- **Trail difficulty:** Easy to moderate.

- **Highlights:** Panoramic views, peaceful trails, and links to local literary history.

- **Duration:** 2-6 hours, depending on the route.

- **Cost:** Free.

Best Parks in Marseille

Marseille is home to several lush parks perfect for picnicking, leisurely walks, or just soaking up the sun.

1. Parc Borély:

This sprawling park near the coast is ideal for a relaxed day outdoors. With its formal gardens, boating lake, and botanical garden, Parc Borély is a favorite among locals and tourists alike.

- **Features:** Boat rentals, cycling paths, and botanical gardens.

- **Entry cost:** Free.

- **Hours:** Open from sunrise to sunset.

- **Highlight:** Its close proximity to the beach makes it easy to combine a park visit with a swim.

2. Parc Longchamp:

Centered around the majestic Palais Longchamp, this historic park offers formal gardens, fountains, and walking paths.

- **Features:** Playgrounds, monuments, and quiet walking paths.

- **Entry cost:** Free (museum entry costs extra).

- **Hours:** Open daily from 7:00 am to 8:00 pm.

- **Highlight:** The beautiful architecture and serene atmosphere.

3. Parc du 26ème Centenaire:

Created to celebrate Marseille's 2,600-year history, this park features gardens themed around various continents and a peaceful pond, making it a great spot for families.

- **Features:** Themed gardens (Provençal, African, Asian), fountains, and play areas.

- **Entry cost:** Free.

- **Hours:** 8:00 am to 6:00 pm (later in summer).

- **Highlight:** A blend of cultures and tranquil green spaces.

Best Views in Marseille

Marseille is famed for its spectacular viewpoints. Here are the top spots for panoramic vistas:

1. Basilique Notre-Dame de la Garde:

Perched high above the city, this iconic basilica offers sweeping views over Marseille, including the Old Port and the Mediterranean Sea.

- **Best time to visit:** Late afternoon, especially for sunset.

- **How to get there:** Bus 60 or a 30-minute uphill walk from the Vieux-Port.

- **Cost:** Free entry.

2. Corniche Kennedy:

This scenic road runs along the coastline, providing picturesque views of the Mediterranean and Marseille's beaches. Several viewpoints along the route offer stunning photo opportunities.

- **Best time to visit:** Early morning or late afternoon for quieter walks.

- **Cost:** Free.

3. Palais du Pharo:

Located at the entrance of the Old Port, the Palais du Pharo's gardens provide stunning views of the Vieux-Port and the city skyline.

- **Best time to visit:** Anytime during daylight hours.

- **Cost:** Free entry to the gardens.

Scenic Spots in Marseille

For beautiful, Instagram-worthy moments, Marseille is full of scenic locations:

1. Vallon des Auffes:

This picturesque fishing port, nestled beneath a stone bridge, is perfect for a tranquil evening stroll or a romantic dinner by the water.

- **Best time to visit:** Evening, when the lights shimmer on the water.

- **Highlight:** The charming fishing boats and waterside restaurants.

2. Îles du Frioul:

A short boat ride from the Vieux-Port takes you to the Frioul Islands, known for their stunning coastal scenery and peaceful beaches.

- **Best time to visit:** Summer, for swimming and hiking.

- **Boat cost:** €10-€12 round trip.

3. Parc National des Calanques:

This park offers not only incredible hiking but also some of the most breathtaking coastal views. Famous Calanques like En-Vau, Morgiou, and Sormiou are all must-sees.

- **Best time to visit:** Spring and autumn for cooler temperatures.

- **Highlight:** Limestone cliffs and pristine waters.

Can You Swim in the Calanques?

Yes! The Calanques are home to some of the best swimming spots in the region, with their clear, calm waters.

Best Calanques for Swimming:

1. Calanque d'En-Vau:

A stunning pebble beach set against towering cliffs, it's a favorite for swimmers.

- **Access:** A 90-minute hike from Cassis or by boat.

- **Tip:** Arrive early to avoid the summer crowds.

2. Calanque de Sormiou:

One of the largest Calanques, it offers sandy beaches and shallow waters, ideal for a day of swimming.

- **Access:** By car or a short hike.

- **Tip:** The road is closed in summer, so plan to walk in.

3. Calanque de Morgiou:

With calm, turquoise waters, Morgiou is less crowded than En-Vau, providing a more peaceful swimming experience.

- **Access:** A 45-minute hike from Luminy.

Swimming Tips:

- **Best time:** Late spring to early autumn.

- **What to bring:** Sunscreen, water shoes, and plenty of water.

- **Note:** Some Calanques may have summer access restrictions due to fire risk, so check the park's website before visiting.

Chapter 13: Marseille for Different Types of Travelers

Marseille's dynamic blend of history, culture, and nature offers something for every type of traveler. Whether you're on a family vacation, a solo journey, a romantic retreat, or a budget trip, this city can cater to your needs with unique and engaging experiences.

Family-Friendly Activities in Marseille

Marseille is a welcoming destination for families, offering activities that entertain both adults and children. From interactive museums to outdoor parks and boat rides, there's plenty to enjoy.

1. Mucem (Museum of European and Mediterranean Civilisations): Families can explore interactive exhibits on Mediterranean history and culture, with stunning rooftop views of the sea.

- **Cost**: €11 for adults, free for children under 18.
- **Highlight**: Kids love the hands-on exhibits, and parents enjoy the panoramic rooftop views.

2. Parc Borély: This coastal park features a lake for boat rentals, wide lawns for picnics, and a botanical garden, making it ideal for family outings.

- **Cost**: Free.
- **Highlight**: Renting rowboats (€3 for 30 minutes) is a hit with kids.

3. La Ferme Pédagogique: Families with younger children will enjoy this educational farm, where kids can interact with animals like goats, chickens, and donkeys.

- **Cost**: Free.
- **Highlight**: Kids love getting hands-on with the animals.

4. Marseille Aquarium (Palais de la Mer): Though small, this aquarium showcases Mediterranean marine life and features interactive exhibits perfect for curious young minds.

- **Cost**: €6 for adults, €3 for children.
- **Highlight**: The touch pools and vibrant sea life displays.

5. Hop-On Hop-Off Bus Tour: Explore Marseille's main attractions at your own pace with this convenient option, great for families with young children.

- **Cost**: €19 for adults, €10 for children.
- **Highlight**: Easily visit top landmarks like Notre-Dame de la Garde and the Old Port.

Solo Travel to Marseille

Marseille offers a fantastic solo travel experience, blending vibrant urban scenes with peaceful nature escapes. Whether you're in the mood to meet new people or enjoy time alone, Marseille has something to offer.

1. Explore Le Panier District: Wander through the artistic, historic Le Panier neighborhood, filled with charming streets, murals, and cozy cafés.

- **Cost**: Free.
- **Highlight**: Solo travelers love the creative atmosphere and the opportunity for people-watching.

2. Join a Walking Tour: Connect with other travelers on a guided walking tour, learning about the city's history or indulging in local cuisine.

- **Cost**: Free tours (suggested tip €10-€15), or paid tours starting at €20.
- **Highlight**: A great way to meet fellow travelers and get insider tips.

3. Hiking in the Calanques: Spend the day hiking in Calanques National Park, where you can enjoy the solitude of nature along with breathtaking views.

- **Cost**: Free.
- **Highlight**: Peaceful trails that allow for reflection and stunning coastal scenery.

4. Visit Cours Julien: As Marseille's hip artistic district, Cours Julien is the perfect place for solo travelers to explore street art, grab a coffee, or shop for unique souvenirs.

- **Cost**: Free to explore, with food and drinks starting around €10.
- **Highlight**: A vibrant neighborhood with a creative vibe and friendly locals.

5. Marseille City Pass: Ideal for solo travelers, the Marseille City Pass offers free entry to museums, boat trips, and unlimited public transport.

- **Cost**: €29 for a 24-hour pass.
- **Highlight**: It provides flexibility and savings for exploring Marseille's attractions.

Romantic Things to Do in Marseille

Marseille offers a variety of romantic experiences, from candlelit dinners by the harbor to scenic sunset spots. The city's coastal charm, rich history, and excellent cuisine make it perfect for couples seeking a romantic getaway.

1. Sunset at Basilique Notre-Dame de la Garde: This iconic basilica offers breathtaking panoramic views, especially stunning at sunset.

- **Cost**: Free.
- **Best time**: Visit at sunset for a romantic, unforgettable view of the city and the sea.

2. Dinner by the Vieux-Port: Enjoy fresh seafood or Mediterranean cuisine at one of the many restaurants overlooking the Old Port.

- **Cost**: A romantic dinner for two with wine ranges from €50-€100.
- **Highlight**: Dining by the glowing lights of the harbor.

3. Boat Trip to Îles du Frioul: Escape the city for a day and enjoy the peaceful, scenic Îles du Frioul, perfect for a romantic picnic or swim.

- **Cost**: Around €12 per person for a round trip.
- **Highlight**: The secluded beaches and clear blue waters.

4. Wine Tasting Tour in Provence: Couples can take a romantic day trip to the Provence region, enjoying vineyard tours and wine tasting.

- **Cost**: Tours start around €60 per person.
- **Highlight**: Sipping local wines together in picturesque Provençal vineyards.

5. Stroll Along the Corniche Kennedy: This scenic road offers stunning views of the Mediterranean, perfect for a romantic evening walk.

- **Cost**: Free.
- **Highlight**: Watching the sunset over the sea hand-in-hand.

Budget Travel in Marseille

Marseille is surprisingly budget-friendly, offering numerous free or low-cost attractions. With affordable dining options and great deals on transport, the city is a great destination for travelers on a budget.

1. Free Walking Tours: Discover Marseille's history and culture through a free walking tour, which operates on a tip-based system.

- **Cost**: Suggested tip €10-€15.
- **Highlight**: A budget-friendly way to learn about the city's history.

2. Visit the Old Port (Vieux-Port): Stroll around the lively Vieux-Port, watch the fishermen at work, and admire the boats—completely free.

- **Cost**: Free.
- **Highlight**: The lively, photogenic atmosphere.

3. Eat at Local Markets: Sample fresh produce and local street food at markets like Marché des Capucins or Marché de Noailles.

- **Cost**: Meals from €5-€10.
- **Highlight**: Tasting authentic Marseille flavors at an affordable price.

4. Marseille City Pass: Save money with the Marseille City Pass, which covers public transport, museums, and boat trips.

- **Cost**: €29 for 24 hours.
- **Highlight**: A fantastic deal for budget-conscious travelers.

5. Relax at Plage des Catalans: Marseille's central beach, Plage des Catalans, is free to access and a perfect spot for sunbathing and swimming.

- **Cost**: Free.

- **Highlight**: Enjoying a relaxing day by the Mediterranean for no cost.

Chapter 14: Cultural Events and Festivals in Marseille

Marseille is a vibrant city steeped in cultural heritage and artistic expression. It offers an eclectic mix of events and festivals throughout the year, showcasing everything from traditional celebrations to cutting-edge contemporary art. With its unique blend of Mediterranean, European, and global influences, Marseille's events calendar is sure to captivate all types of travelers.

Marseille Events Calendar

Marseille hosts a diverse range of annual events that celebrate the city's musical, artistic, and cultural traditions. Below are some of the most significant events:

1. Fête de la Musique (June 21st): A nationwide celebration, this event turns Marseille into a giant open-air concert hall. Musicians of all genres fill the streets, parks, and public squares, offering everything from classical music to jazz, hip-hop, and rock.

- **Location**: Various venues across the city.
- **Cost**: Free.
- **Highlight**: Discover local and international music in a festive outdoor atmosphere.

2. Festival de Marseille (June - July): This celebration of contemporary art features dance, theater, music, and visual arts from around the world. Performances and exhibitions are hosted in venues across the city, from museums to open spaces.

- **Location**: Various venues, including theaters and museums.
- **Cost**: Ticket prices range from free to €30, depending on the event.
- **Highlight**: A dynamic mix of avant-garde performances and interactive exhibits.

3. Marseille Jazz des Cinq Continents (July): A prestigious international jazz festival, this event draws renowned musicians from around the globe. Concerts are held in stunning outdoor locations such as the historic Parc Longchamp.

- **Location**: Parc Longchamp and other venues.
- **Cost**: Tickets range from €20 to €50.
- **Highlight**: World-class jazz performances in picturesque settings.

4. Fiesta des Suds (October): Celebrating world music and global cultures, this lively festival features artists from diverse genres, including reggae, electronic,

Latin, and African music. The festival also offers food stalls, dance performances, and cultural exhibitions.

- **Location**: Dock des Suds and other waterfront venues.
- **Cost**: Tickets range from €25 to €45.
- **Highlight**: A colorful, immersive cultural experience with music from across the globe.

5. Christmas Markets (December): During the holiday season, Marseille's streets are transformed with twinkling lights and festive markets. The main market at the Vieux-Port offers everything from Provençal products to local handicrafts and traditional holiday treats.

- **Location**: Vieux-Port and other central areas.
- **Cost**: Free entry, with products starting at €5.
- **Highlight**: A charming festive atmosphere and delicious holiday treats.

Cultural Events in Marseille

In addition to its annual festivals, Marseille also hosts numerous cultural events that highlight its Mediterranean roots, maritime history, and artistic evolution.

1. Carnaval de Marseille (February - March): This lively pre-Lenten celebration sees the streets come alive with music, dancers, and colorful costumes. Local communities participate in parades through the city, culminating in a grand party at Vieux-Port.

- **Location**: Main streets, including La Canebière and Vieux-Port.
- **Cost**: Free.
- **Highlight**: The exuberant parade, featuring elaborate floats and costumes.

2. Fête du Panier (June): This neighborhood festival celebrates Le Panier, one of Marseille's oldest districts. Visitors can enjoy live performances, art installations, and street food, all set against the backdrop of historic Marseille.

- **Location**: Le Panier district.
- **Cost**: Free.
- **Highlight**: A vibrant community event that showcases the local artistic and cultural scene.

3. Festival International du Film de Marseille (FIDMarseille) (July): A major event for film lovers, this international festival focuses on documentary and experimental films. It brings together filmmakers, critics, and audiences for screenings, workshops, and discussions.

- **Location**: Various cinemas, including Alcazar Library and Théâtre de La Criée.
- **Cost**: Tickets range from €5 to €10.
- **Highlight**: Unique and thought-provoking independent films.

4. Journées du Patrimoine (European Heritage Days) (September): Each year, Marseille's historic sites open their doors to the public for free, offering guided tours and special access to monuments like Notre-Dame de la Garde, Palais Longchamp, and Fort Saint-Jean.

- **Location**: Historic sites across the city.
- **Cost**: Free entry.
- **Highlight**: Access to normally closed-off parts of historic buildings.

5. Feria de Marseille (April): Inspired by Southern French and Spanish traditions, the Feria de Marseille offers flamenco performances, bullfighting demonstrations (non-lethal), and Andalusian music and dance, transforming the city into a lively fiesta.

- **Location**: Parc Chanot and various public squares.
- **Cost**: Free to attend.
- **Highlight**: The lively Andalusian music and vibrant flamenco performances.

Art Galleries in Marseille

Marseille is home to a rich selection of art galleries, offering everything from classical masterpieces to contemporary works by local and international artists.

1. Musée Cantini Specializing in modern and contemporary art, the Musée Cantini features works by some of the 20th century's most influential artists, including Picasso, Matisse, and Léger.

- **Entry cost**: €6 for adults, free for children under 18.
- **Highlight**: A stunning collection of 20th-century art housed in a historic mansion.

2. La Friche la Belle de Mai A former tobacco factory turned cultural center, La Friche is home to contemporary art exhibitions, theater performances, concerts, and a popular rooftop terrace with panoramic views of the city.

- **Entry cost**: Free for most exhibitions, event tickets from €10.
- **Highlight**: A creative space where art, music, and culture converge.

3. Galerie Polysémie Known for its focus on outsider art, Galerie Polysémie showcases unconventional and thought-provoking works from self-taught artists, offering a unique perspective on the art world.

- **Entry cost**: Free.
- **Highlight**: A one-of-a-kind collection of Art Brut and outsider art.

4. MAC – Musée d'Art Contemporain de Marseille Located near the beach, this contemporary art museum features works from the 1960s to the present day, with a focus on French and international contemporary artists.

- **Entry cost**: €9 for adults, free for students and children under 18.
- **Highlight**: Innovative and rotating exhibitions that push artistic boundaries.

5. Fonds Régional d'Art Contemporain Provence-Alpes-Côte d'Azur (FRAC PACA) A major hub for contemporary art, FRAC PACA hosts rotating exhibitions of modern art, with a focus on avant-garde installations and interactive displays.

- **Entry cost**: €6 for adults, free for children under 18.
- **Highlight**: Cutting-edge exhibitions and immersive installations.

Chapter 15: Getting Around Marseille

Marseille is a sprawling, bustling city, but thanks to its well-structured transportation network, navigating the city is both easy and convenient. Whether you're hopping on a metro, taking a scenic ferry ride, or renting a bike to explore the city's hills and coastline, Marseille has a transportation option to suit every traveler.

Public Transportation in Marseille

Marseille boasts an efficient public transportation system managed by the RTM (Régie des Transports Métropolitains), offering a seamless network of metros, buses, and trams that connect different parts of the city.

1. Metro Marseille's two metro lines, **M1** and **M2**, are the fastest way to travel through the city, connecting key districts and landmarks. Both lines operate from early morning until after midnight.

- **Operating hours**: 5:00 AM – 12:30 AM.
- **Cost**: €1.90 per single ticket, valid for 1 hour across all RTM transportation.
- **Metro highlights**: Line 1 runs from **La Rose** to **La Fourragère**, passing through the city center,

while Line 2 runs from **Bougainville** to **Sainte-Marguerite Dromel**, covering key areas of the city.

2. Buses Marseille has a vast bus network that covers the entire city and nearby suburbs. With over 80 bus routes, buses are a convenient option for areas not covered by the metro.

- **Cost**: €1.90 per trip (or free with the **Marseille City Pass**).
- **Tip**: Use the **RTM app** for real-time schedules and route planning, especially during off-peak times or Sundays when service may be less frequent.

3. Trams Marseille's three tram lines—**T1**, **T2**, and **T3**—connect various parts of the city center, making it easy to travel between neighborhoods like Noailles, Longchamp, and Les Caillols.

- **Cost**: Same fare as metro and buses—€1.90 per trip.
- **Highlights**: The tram offers a scenic way to navigate the city's central areas.

4. Day Passes If you plan to use public transportation frequently during your stay, day passes offer excellent value.

- **Prices**: €5.50 for a 24-hour pass, €10 for a 3-day pass.
- **Benefits**: Unlimited travel on metro, buses, and trams.

Marseille City Pass

The **Marseille City Pass** is ideal for tourists who want to explore the city's top attractions while enjoying unlimited public transport.

Key Features:

- Unlimited use of metro, bus, tram, and boat shuttle.

- Free or discounted entry to museums like **MuCEM** and **Musée Cantini**.

- Free boat trips to the **Frioul Islands** or **Château d'If**.

- Free guided walking tours and discounts on other tours.

Cost:

- €29 for 24 hours.

- €39 for 48 hours.

- €49 for 72 hours.

Why Get the City Pass? It's a fantastic deal for visitors who plan to visit multiple attractions and take advantage of public transportation. The pass quickly pays for itself, especially if you visit popular spots like **Château d'If** and **MuCEM**.

Marseille Ferry Services

Exploring Marseille by ferry is a delightful way to enjoy the city's Mediterranean coastline while visiting nearby islands. Ferries connect different parts of the city as well as nearby islands such as the **Îles du Frioul** and **Château d'If**.

1. Vieux-Port to Îles du Frioul This ferry departs from the iconic **Old Port** and takes you to the **Îles du Frioul**, a group of serene islands known for their beaches and hiking trails.

- **Schedule**: Ferries run every 1-2 hours depending on the season.
- **Cost**: Round trip costs between €10-€15.

- **Tip**: Book tickets in advance during summer weekends.

2. Vieux-Port to Château d'If The ferry to the famous **Château d'If**, known from *The Count of Monte Cristo*, departs from the Old Port and reaches the fortress island in about 20 minutes.

- **Schedule**: Ferries run hourly.
- **Cost**: €11 round trip (plus a €6 entrance fee to Château d'If).
- **Tip**: Check the weather—strong winds may cause cancellations.

3. Shuttle Boat Services (Navettes): Marseille also offers shuttle boat services connecting the **northern** and **southern** shores of the city, offering scenic rides and an alternative to road travel.

- **Routes**: **Vieux-Port** to **Pointe-Rouge** and **Vieux-Port** to **L'Estaque**.
- **Cost**: €5 per trip.
- **Tip**: Take a shuttle boat for a relaxing, crowd-free way to enjoy the coastline.

Marseille Bike Rentals

With an increasing number of dedicated bike lanes and scenic cycling routes, renting a bike is a fantastic way to see Marseille at your own pace. Whether exploring the coastal **Corniche** or the historic **Le Panier** district, biking offers both flexibility and fun.

1. Le Vélo (Public Bike Share Program) Le Vélo, Marseille's public bike-share service, has over 1,000 bikes available at 130 docking stations citywide.

- **Cost**: €1 for a day pass, with the first 30 minutes of each ride free. After 30 minutes, it's €1 per additional hour.
- **How it works**: Pick up and return bikes at any docking station. Download the **Le Vélo app** for easy bike tracking and station locations.
- **Tip**: Keep your rides under 30 minutes to avoid extra fees.

2. Private Bike Rentals: For a full-day or multi-day rental, several companies around **Vieux-Port** and the city center offer affordable rates.

- **Cost**: €15-€20 per day.

- **Best routes**: The **Corniche Kennedy** for stunning sea views and **Parc Borély** for a peaceful ride through lush greenery.

3. Electric Bike Rentals: Given Marseille's hilly terrain, electric bikes are an excellent option for those planning to visit elevated areas like **Notre-Dame de la Garde** or the slopes of **Le Panier**.

- **Cost**: €25-€35 per day.
- **Tip**: Guided electric bike tours are available, offering an informative and scenic ride through the city's highlights.

Chapter 16: Essential Travel Tips for Marseille

Before heading to Marseille, it's important to be prepared with some essential tips to make your trip safe, comfortable, and budget-friendly. From safety guidelines to what to pack, here's what you need to know for a smooth visit to this vibrant Mediterranean city.

Is Marseille Safe for Tourists?

Marseille is a lively city, and while most tourist areas are generally safe, some areas can be less secure, especially at night. With basic precautions, you can enjoy Marseille worry-free.

1. Pickpocketing: Like in many big cities, pickpocketing can be an issue in crowded areas, especially on public transport, at markets, or near busy tourist attractions like **La Canebière** and **Vieux-Port**.

- **Tip**: Use a money belt or anti-theft bag, and avoid flashing valuables like expensive cameras or smartphones.

2. Avoid Certain Areas at Night: Some neighborhoods, especially in the northern districts like **Noailles** and **La Castellane**, may feel unsafe at night.

Stick to well-lit, populated areas and avoid wandering alone after dark in unfamiliar places.

3. Local Police Presence: Marseille has an increased police presence in tourist areas, ensuring added security. If you ever feel unsafe, don't hesitate to approach local authorities for help.

Overall Safety Rating: While Marseille may have a reputation for being gritty, most visitors experience a trouble-free stay. With common-sense precautions, you can expect a safe and enjoyable trip.

What to Pack for Marseille

Marseille's Mediterranean climate means hot summers and mild, often unpredictable winters, so it's important to pack according to the season.

1. Lightweight Clothing for Summer With summer temperatures often reaching the high 30s°C (90s°F), pack breathable fabrics like cotton and linen. Don't forget your **sunglasses**, **sunhat**, and **sunscreen** to protect yourself from the intense Mediterranean sun.

2. Layers for Spring and Fall Spring and autumn can bring cooler mornings and warm afternoons, so it's a good idea to pack layers. A **light jacket, sweaters**, and **long-**

sleeved shirts will help keep you comfortable throughout the day.

3. Rain Gear for Winter Winters in Marseille are mild but often rainy. Between November and March, pack a **compact umbrella** and a **waterproof jacket**.

4. Comfortable Walking Shoes The city's cobblestone streets and hilly neighborhoods like **Le Panier** require sturdy, comfortable walking shoes. **Sneakers** or **flat sandals** are ideal for exploring on foot.

5. Beach Essentials If visiting in the summer, pack **swimwear**, **flip-flops**, and a **towel** for beach days. Be sure to bring **reef-safe sunscreen** if you plan to swim in the **Calanques** or around the **Frioul Islands**.

What to Wear in Marseille

Marseille is a laid-back, cosmopolitan city where casual yet fashionable clothing is widely accepted. Knowing what to wear helps you blend in with the locals while staying comfortable in the city's varied climate.

1. Casual Daywear For sightseeing, especially in summer, lightweight and comfortable clothing is key. Locals typically wear **jeans**, **shorts**, **sundresses**, and simple **t-shirts**.

- **Tip**: While shorts are fine for sightseeing, lightweight pants or skirts are more appropriate for visits to churches or museums.

2. Evening Outfits When dining out or exploring Marseille's nightlife, a slightly smarter dress code is common. Men typically wear **shirts with trousers** or dark jeans, while women might opt for **chic dresses** or **blouses with skirts**.

3. Beachwear Etiquette Beach attire is fine at the beach or seaside cafes, but make sure to cover up with a **shirt**, **dress**, or **shorts** when leaving beach areas or using public transportation.

4. Religious Sites When visiting places like the **Basilique Notre-Dame de la Garde**, modest clothing is recommended. Be sure to cover your **shoulders** and **knees** as a sign of respect.

Can You Drink Tap Water in Marseille?

Yes, tap water in Marseille is safe to drink. It meets all French health standards and is sourced from the Durance River, making it clean and refreshing.

- **Tip**: Bring a **refillable water bottle** to save money and reduce plastic waste. Tap water is often served for free in restaurants if requested.

- **Bottled Water**: Some people prefer bottled water, which is available in **still** (eau plate) and **sparkling** (eau gazeuse) varieties. A 1.5-liter bottle typically costs between €0.50 and €1.50 at supermarkets.

Marseille Travel Budget Tips

Compared to cities like Paris and Nice, Marseille is relatively affordable. However, there are plenty of ways to make your trip even more budget-friendly without compromising on experiences.

1. Use Public Transport: Marseille's public transport system is well-connected and affordable, making it easy to explore the city on a budget.

- **Tip**: Buy a **24-hour ticket** for €5.50 or a **3-day pass** for €10 to save on transportation costs.

2. Eat like a Local: Dining in casual eateries or shopping at markets can save you a lot of money. Check out **Marché des Capucins** for affordable, fresh produce, cheese, and bread.

- **Price range**: Street food like sandwiches and **panisses** (chickpea fritters) costs around €3-€6, while casual meals at bistros range from €10 to €20.

3. Explore Free Attractions: Many of Marseille's highlights, such as **Vieux-Port**, **Le Panier**, and **Basilique Notre-Dame de la Garde**, are free to visit. You can also enjoy **hiking in Calanques National Park** or wandering through local parks at no cost.

4. Save with the City Pass: The **Marseille City Pass** offers free public transport, museum entries, and boat trips to **Château d'If** and the **Frioul Islands**. The **72-hour pass** costs €49 and is a great deal if you plan to visit several attractions.

5. Budget Accommodation: Marseille has a range of budget-friendly accommodations, from hostels to affordable hotels.

- **Hostels**: €20-€30 per night for a shared dorm.
- **Budget hotels**: Prices start at €50 per night for a basic room.

6. Visit during the Off-Season: To avoid high prices and crowds, visit in **spring** (April-May) or **autumn**

(September-October). These shoulder seasons offer lower accommodation rates, cheaper flights, and milder weather.

Chapter 17: Sample Itineraries for Marseille

Whether you're spending just one day or enjoying a long weekend, Marseille offers a wide range of experiences, from exploring historical landmarks and scenic views to savoring the city's renowned seafood. Below are sample itineraries designed to help you make the most of your time in this dynamic Mediterranean city.

Weekend in Marseille Itinerary (2 Days)

For a short stay in Marseille, this itinerary covers the city's most iconic sites and provides a taste of the local culture.

Day 1: Discover the Old Town and Seaside Charm

- **Morning**:
  Begin your day at **Vieux-Port (Old Port)**, the heart of Marseille. Stroll along the harbor, where colorful fishing boats dot the water, and visit the lively **Fish Market** to witness fresh catches of the day. Stop at a café for a traditional French breakfast.

  Afterward, head to **Le Panier**, the city's oldest district, known for its winding streets, charming houses, and street art. Visit **La Vieille Charité**, a historic building housing museums and exhibitions.

- o **Tip**: Try a **panisse** (fried chickpea cake) from a street vendor in Le Panier.

- **Lunch**:
  Enjoy a Mediterranean-inspired lunch at **Le Café des Épices**, a bistro near the Old Port. Expect to spend around €20-€30 per person.

- **Afternoon**:
  Take the #60 bus or tourist train up to **Basilique Notre-Dame de la Garde**, Marseille's most iconic landmark. Climb to the top of the basilica for breathtaking views of the city and the Mediterranean Sea.
  Afterward, enjoy a leisurely walk along **Corniche Kennedy**, a scenic coastal road offering stunning sea views.

- **Evening**:
  For dinner, indulge in **bouillabaisse** (fish stew) at **Chez Fonfon**, a seafood restaurant located in **Vallon des Auffes**. A meal here will cost around €40-€60 per person.

Day 2: Exploring History and Nature

- **Morning**:
  Begin with a visit to **MuCEM (Museum of European and Mediterranean Civilizations)** near the Old Port. The museum's exhibits cover Mediterranean history and culture, and the modern architecture is a highlight. Admission is €11.

- Afterward, take a boat from the Old Port to **Château d'If**, the island fortress made famous by *The Count of Monte Cristo*. The ferry ride is about 20 minutes, and a round-trip ticket costs €11. Entry to the château is €6.

- **Lunch**:
  Have lunch at **Le Miramar**, a restaurant near the Old Port specializing in Provençal cuisine. Lunch

- will cost between €20 and €40 per person.

- **Afternoon**:
  Head to **Calanques National Park** for an afternoon of hiking. Take a bus or drive to **Cassis**, about 30 minutes from Marseille. Explore the scenic **Calanque de Port-Miou** or **Calanque d'En-Vau**, known for their turquoise waters and

limestone cliffs. Bring plenty of water and wear sturdy shoes.

- **Evening**:
  Wrap up your weekend with a relaxing evening in **Le Panier** or **Cours Julien**, areas known for street art and laid-back nightlife. Enjoy dinner at **La Cantinetta**, an Italian-Mediterranean restaurant, where meals cost around €25-€35 per person.

How to Spend 3 Days in Marseille

With three days, you'll have more time to explore Marseille's diverse neighborhoods, culture, and natural surroundings. Here's how to make the most of your extended stay.

Day 1: Classic Marseille

- Begin your morning exploring **Vieux-Port** and **Le Panier**.

- In the afternoon, visit **MuCEM** and **Fort Saint-Jean**. Take a walk along **Corniche Kennedy** for stunning sea views.

- End the day with a seafood dinner at **Chez Fonfon**.

Day 2: Culture and Calanques

- Start your morning at **Basilique Notre-Dame de la Garde**.

- In the afternoon, take a boat to **Château d'If** or explore the **Frioul Islands**.

- Enjoy dinner in **Le Panier** or along the waterfront.

Day 3: Day Trip to Cassis and Calanques

- Spend the day exploring **Calanques National Park** by boat or on foot.

- Have a leisurely lunch in **Cassis** before returning to Marseille for the evening in the **Cours Julien** district, known for its relaxed atmosphere and vibrant nightlife.

What to See in Marseille in a Day

Even with just one day in Marseille, you can experience some of the city's most iconic sites.

Morning:

Start at **Vieux-Port**, soaking up the lively atmosphere and visiting the local fish market. From here, wander the streets of **Le Panier**, Marseille's oldest neighborhood, visiting **La Vieille Charité** and admiring the colorful street art.

Lunch:

For lunch, enjoy a seafood meal at **Le Miramar** near the Old Port. A high-quality meal, including **bouillabaisse**, costs around €40-€60 per person.

Afternoon:

After lunch, take the bus or tourist train to **Basilique Notre-Dame de la Garde** for panoramic views of the city.

From there, head back to the waterfront to explore **MuCEM** and **Fort Saint-Jean**. Even if you don't enter the museum, the views from the rooftop and fort are worth a visit.

Evening:

End your day with a stroll along **Corniche Kennedy**, enjoying the sea breeze and watching the sunset over the Mediterranean.

What to Do in Marseille in 2 Days

Two days in Marseille allows you to see the major highlights and enjoy the city's laid-back atmosphere.

Day 1: Iconic Landmarks

- **Morning**: Explore **Vieux-Port** and **Le Panier**.

- **Afternoon**: Visit **MuCEM, Fort Saint-Jean,** and **Basilique Notre-Dame de la Garde**.

- **Evening**: Dine at a seafood restaurant like **Chez Fonfon**.

Day 2: Calanques and Coastal Beauty

- **Morning**: Hike or take a boat tour in **Calanques National Park**, starting from **Cassis**.

- **Afternoon**: Explore **Cassis**, then return to Marseille for the evening.

- **Evening**: Enjoy dinner at **La Cantinetta** or in **Cours Julien**.

Conclusion

Marseille, a city where history, culture, and coastal beauty converge, offers an unforgettable travel experience. Whether you're strolling through its vibrant districts, savoring fresh seafood, or hiking the rugged Calanques, this Mediterranean port city truly has something for everyone. To wrap up your journey, here are some final travel tips and a summary of the must-visit spots that will make your trip to Marseille truly memorable.

Final Travel Tips for Marseille

1. **Plan Your Visits to Key Attractions in Advance**: Marseille's top attractions, such as **MuCEM** and **Basilique Notre-Dame de la Garde**, can become crowded, especially during peak tourist seasons. Booking tickets in advance can save you from long lines. If you're visiting during the summer, arriving early helps you avoid both the crowds and the midday heat.

2. **Stay Hydrated and Protect Yourself from the Sun**: With summer temperatures often exceeding 30°C (86°F), it's important to carry water and protect yourself from the sun. Always have sunscreen and a hat, especially if you're

spending time outdoors or hiking in **Calanques National Park**. Drinking fountains can be found throughout the city for refills.

3. **Use Public Transportation Efficiently** Marseille's public transport system, run by RTM, includes buses, trams, and a metro. The **Marseille City Pass** is a great deal if you're visiting multiple attractions, offering free transportation and entry to many sites. A 24-hour pass costs €27, and a 72-hour pass is €43.

4. **Stay Aware of Your Surroundings**: Marseille is generally safe, but like any large city, it's wise to be cautious in busy tourist spots and on public transport. Keep an eye on your belongings, and avoid poorly lit or unfamiliar streets, particularly at night around the **Vieux-Port**.

5. **Embrace Local Customs**: Marseille has a rich Provençal and Mediterranean culture. Take time to appreciate the local customs, such as greeting people with "Bonjour" when entering shops or restaurants. Don't miss the chance to try **bouillabaisse**, the city's signature fish stew, or sip on **Pastis**, a local anise-flavored spirit.

Summary of Must-Visit Places in Marseille

1. **Vieux-Port (Old Port)**: The heart of the city and a great starting point for any Marseille adventure. Soak in the lively atmosphere, visit the famous Fish Market, and indulge in fresh seafood at the many restaurants.

2. **Le Panier**: Marseille's oldest district is famous for its narrow streets, colorful facades, and street art. Be sure to visit **La Vieille Charité**, a stunning architectural gem that houses museums and galleries.

3. **Basilique Notre-Dame de la Garde**: This iconic basilica offers breathtaking panoramic views of the city and the sea. It's one of Marseille's most beloved landmarks and is accessible by bus, train, or on foot.

4. **MuCEM (Museum of European and Mediterranean Civilizations)**: Situated near the Old Port, this museum is a must for history buffs and culture lovers. Its striking modern architecture and stunning waterfront location make it a highlight of the city.

5. **Calanques National Park**: For nature lovers, a day trip to **Calanques National Park** is a must. Whether you hike or take a boat tour, the park's dramatic cliffs and turquoise waters are simply awe-inspiring.

6. **Château d'If**: Known from **The Count of Monte Cristo**, this island fortress is accessible by boat from the Old Port. Explore its storied history and take in the beautiful coastal views along the way.

7. **Cours Julien**: A vibrant district filled with street art, quirky shops, and lively bars. If you're into Marseille's alternative culture, this is the place to be.

8. **Corniche Kennedy**: This scenic coastal road offers some of the best views of the Mediterranean. Perfect for an evening walk, it's an ideal spot to catch a sunset and soak in the beauty of the city.

Final Thoughts

Marseille's unique blend of history, culture, and stunning natural landscapes makes it a must-visit destination for travelers of all kinds. From wandering through historic streets and bustling markets to gazing at the spectacular views of the Calanques and the Mediterranean, there is always something to discover. With these tips and itineraries, you'll be well-prepared to immerse yourself in all that this fascinating city has to offer. Whether it's your first visit or a return trip, Marseille promises a memorable and enriching experience in the heart of Provence.

Maps

Map of Marseille

https://maps.app.goo.gl/c1Ta9yhvS4tZZ4XP8

SCAN IMAGE OF THE QR CODE WITH YOUR PHONE

TO GET LOCATION IN REAL TIME

Map of Things to do

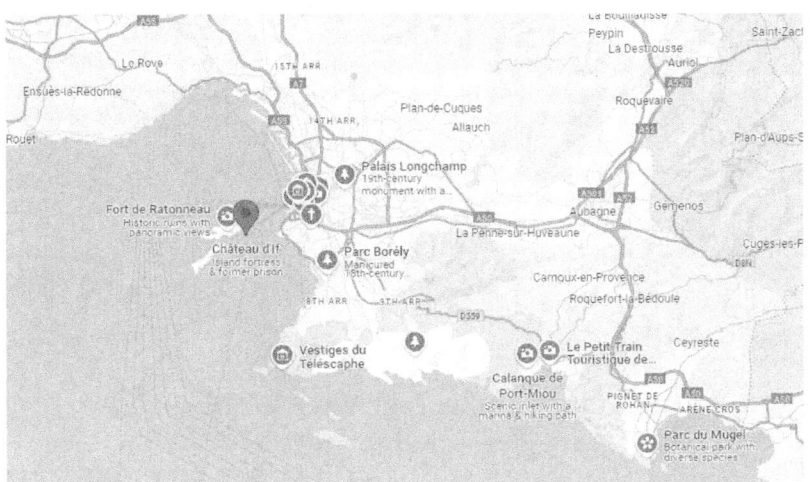

https://maps.app.goo.gl/4cX2paCe9HFdj3ND6

SCAN IMAGE OF THE QR CODE WITH YOUR PHONE

TO GET LOCATION IN REAL TIME

Maps of Restaurants

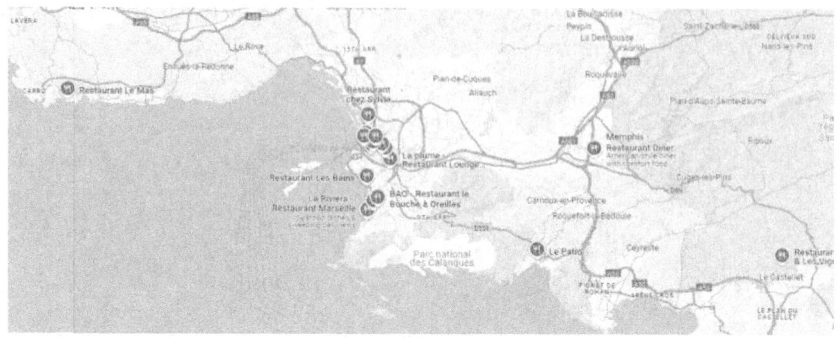

https://maps.app.goo.gl/v6yL5oZPEzegJ55e7

SCAN IMAGE OF THE QR CODE WITH YOUR PHONE

TO GET LOCATION IN REAL TIME

Map of Museums

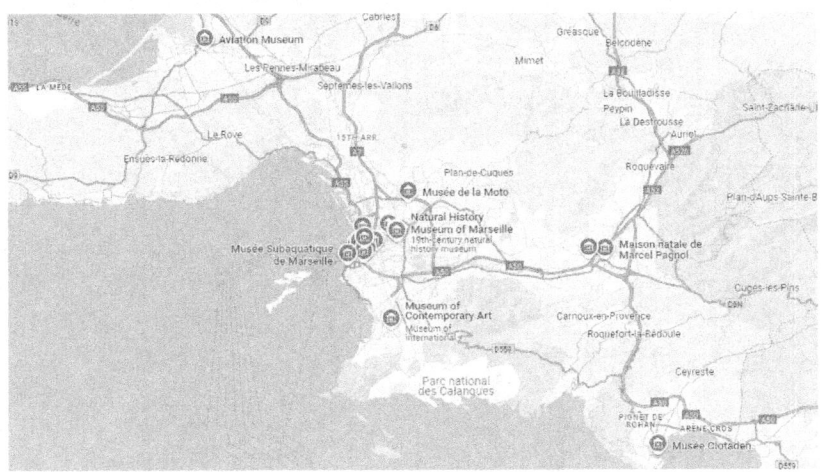

https://maps.app.goo.gl/sQ3PsoWxm1wKa7Xf9

SCAN IMAGE OF THE QR
CODE WITH YOUR PHONE

TO GET LOCATION IN
REAL TIME

Map of Transits Stations

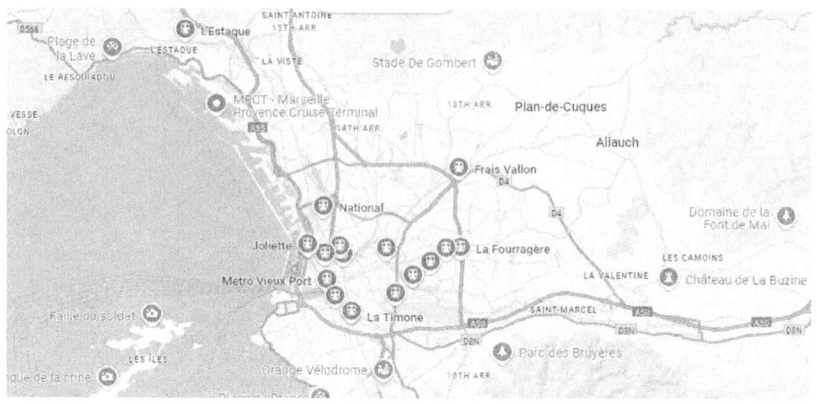

https://maps.app.goo.gl/eSYRkb5HijkNfuzKA

SCAN IMAGE OF THE QR CODE WITH YOUR PHONE

TO GET LOCATION IN REAL TIME

Map of Pharmacies

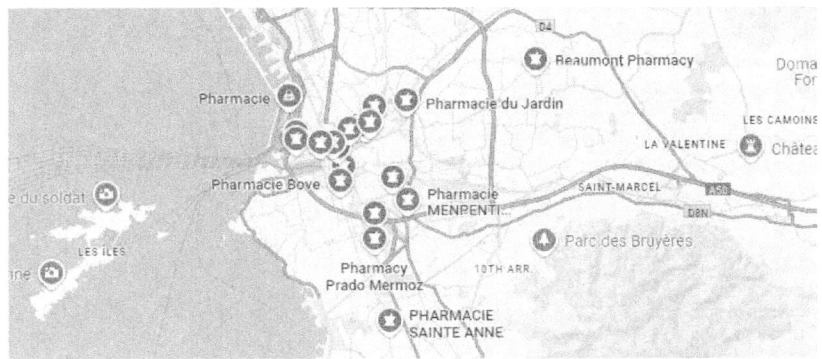

https://maps.app.goo.gl/EtkJ1bdBYkRVyDDC7

SCAN IMAGE OF THE QR CODE WITH YOUR PHONE

TO GET LOCATION IN REAL TIME

Map of ATM Spots

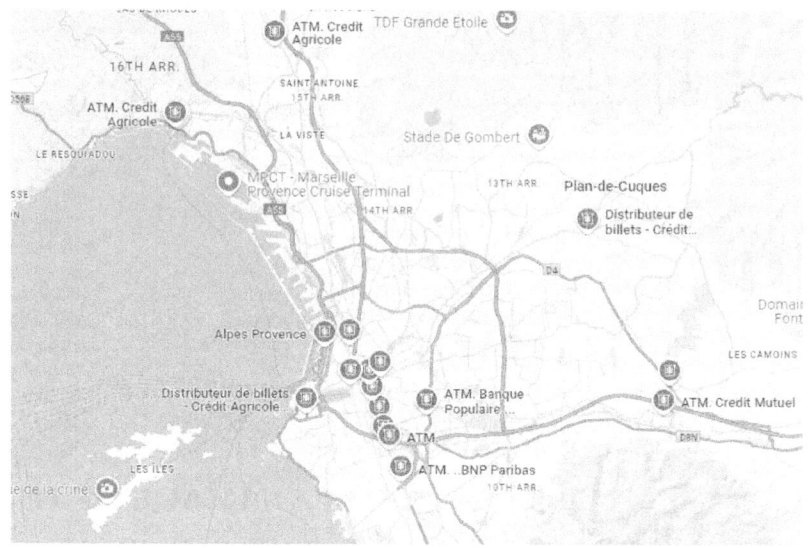

https://maps.app.goo.gl/JqLe5vSfYQiaKsPq6

SCAN IMAGE OF THE QR CODE WITH YOUR PHONE

TO GET LOCATION IN REAL TIME

Printed in Great Britain
by Amazon